EASY
THAI
COOKBOOK

EASY
THAI
COOKBOOK

THE STEP-BY-STEP GUIDE TO DELICIOUSLY EASY THAI FOOD AT HOME

SALLIE MORRIS

METRO BOOKS
NEW YORK

Managing Editor: Grace Cheetham
Editors: Gillian Haslam and Alison Bolus
Managing Designer: Manisha Patel
Designer: Sailesh Patel
Studio Photography: William Lingwood
Photography Assistant: Alice Deuchar
Stylists: Jenny White (food) and Helen Trent (props)

Metro Books
122 Fifth Avenue
New York, NY 10011

ISBN: 978-1-4351-2121-8

Printed and bound in Singapore

10 9 8 7 6 5 4 3 2 1

To Johnnie, who has had patience above and beyond and
who loves Thai food.

Author's acknowledgments

Thanks to the following organizations, hotels, restaurants, and
individuals: In Bangkok, Khun Kurt Wachtveitl and Khun Mayuree
(Oriental Hotel); Khun Chalie Amatyukul; Khun Naroor Somany-Steppe
and Carl Steppe (The Blue Elephant Cookery School). In Chiang Mai,
Khun Mem (Mandarin Oriental Dhara Devi Cookery School) and the
River View Lodge. In Phuket, Khun Tom Navanukroh and Duang Thip
(Cape Panwa Hotel). In the UK, Khun Nan Ratanarat and his wife
Sunanta (The Golden Fleece, Elstead, Surrey), whose help with many
recipes was invaluable; Magimix, for the best food processor and steamer;
The Montien Restaurant, Kew, Surrey; Phalida (Paya Thai Supermarket,
Richmond, Surrey); Monsoon Wines; Eva Air (Taiwanese airline);
Richard Hume (Thai Tourist Office); and Beryl Castles. Finally, Grace
Cheetham from Duncan Baird Publishers for all her support.

Publisher's note

While every care has been taken in compiling the recipes for this book,
Duncan Baird Publishers, or any other persons who have been involved
in working on this publication, cannot accept responsibility for any
errors or omissions, inadvertent or not, that may be found in the recipes
or text, nor for any problems that may arise as a result of preparing one
of these recipes. If you are pregnant or breastfeeding or have any special
dietary requirements or medical conditions, it is advisable to consult a
medical professional before following any of the recipes contained in
this book.

Notes on the recipes

Unless otherwise stated:
• Use medium eggs
• Use fresh herbs
• 1 tsp = 5ml
  1 tbsp = 15ml
  1 cup = 240ml

Language notes

English and Thai names are used throughout the book. There is no
definitive way to translate spellings from Thai to English because Thai
is tonal. *Nam* can be *nahm*, *phed* can be *phet*, and *tom khaa gai* can be *tom ga khai*.
If in doubt, say the word out loud.

CONTENTS

INTRODUCTION

The popularity of Thai food is borne out by the ever-increasing number of Thai restaurants, as more people recognize the delicious mouth-tingling delights of real Thai cuisine. Originally the Thai (Tai) people were migrants from southwest China who first settled in the north and kept moving southward, setting up capitals with romantic names such as Sukhothai ("Dawn of Happiness"), Ayutthaya ("Unassailable"), and then Bangkok ("City of Angels") at the end of the eighteenth century. On their move south, they found that the fertile central plains and plentiful rainfall proved perfect for paddy fields of superb quality, which is why the area is known as the rice bowl of Southeast Asia.

Thailand is about the size of France with a population of around 60 million. Burma, Laos, Cambodia, and Malaysia are its immediate neighbors. With trade between these and other countries of the region, many ingredients are common to each cuisine but are frequently employed in entirely different cooking methods, neatly illustrating the point that food has no borders or boundaries. Though regional cooking exists in Thailand, Thai restaurants will more usually cook and serve the better known dishes that they know their customers will enjoy.

The development of Thai cuisine, with its historical and culinary influences from China, has been a long and subtle process. From Arab and Indian merchants, the Thais adopted the use of dry spices—coriander, cumin, nutmeg, cloves, and turmeric—as used in the Thai Mussaman Curry (see page 98). This gave a new dimension to the work of the talented cooks of the royal household that eventually developed into what is today one of the world's most exciting cuisines. Perhaps the most significant import was the chili, which was brought east by the Portuguese. Its place in the cooking of Thailand is undisputed, but it is the clever way in which the different flavors are married together that makes Thai food unique. Threads of Indian cuisine are also revealed in the rich tapestry of Thai food. The wet spice pastes bear a strong resemblance to the masalas of southern India that invariably include the essential three Cs of oriental cooking: coconut, chili, and cilantro.

The three overriding attractions of Thai food are the tastes, the textures, and the aromas. The tastes include red and green hot bird's eye chilies; creamy coconut; cilantro (roots, stalks, and leaves); basil leaves, with their aniseed aroma; heavenly lemongrass; pine-like kha; torn lime leaves (just smell that citrus fragrance); limes for their juice or as wedges to squeeze over prepared dishes; pungent kapi (fermented shrimp paste), which has no fishy taste but gives depth to dishes in which it is used; and salty, whiskey-colored fish sauce, *nam pla*—definitely *the* Thai condiment. The textures are crunchy peanuts and toasted dried coconut (unsweetened), crisp green vegetables and unripe fruits for salads such as green mango, meltingly tender deep-fried fish and curried meats, and juicy, simply prepared oriental fruits, such as mangosteens and lychees. As for the aromas, just the fragrance of lemongrass and lime leaves or the aroma of a curry paste being stirred into coconut milk is enough to whet the appetite.

An interest in food is always a joy—a never-ending voyage of discovery in which there is always something new around the corner. With the growing popularity of Thai cuisine, the ingredients are increasingly widely available, whether in supermarkets or delis, so, with the help of these recipes, you too can cook authentic Thai food.

PART 1

THE BASICS

*Thai cuisine involves **ingredients** that may be unfamiliar to some cooks, but virtually all of them will be available from large **supermarkets**, if you are not lucky enough to have an **oriental** store near you. Bamboo shoots, bean curd, bean sprouts, chilies, **coconut**, curry pastes, fish sauce, and lemongrass all add their exotic flavors to Thai meals. **Rice** and food are synonymous in the Thai language, so a good helping of rice is central to the meal, unless **noodles** are being served.*

*The only specialist equipment you will need is a **wok** for stir-fries, though a mortar and pestle are useful for grinding **pastes**. Thai food is usually barbecued, deep-fried, steamed, or stir-fried, all of which are **quick** methods of cooking, so the food will be ready in no time. Only **curries**, which need to simmer for a while to develop their **flavors**, take much time to cook. At the heart of Thai cooking lie the pastes on which so many **delicious** dishes are based: red and green curry pastes, Mussaman curry paste, and Hung Lay curry paste all play an **important** part in the final flavor, though many have their **spicy** character subdued by the addition of **coconut** milk—a central ingredient in Thai food. Once you understand the basic ingredients and methods, you are ready to **prepare** your first Thai meal.*

INGREDIENTS

BAMBOO SHOOTS

Sliced bamboo shoots are available in cans. Once the can is opened, pour the contents into a container with a lid, cover with fresh water daily, and use within a week.

BANANA LEAVES

These giant leaves are available from some oriental supermarkets. Plunge the leaves into boiling water to make them more supple before placing the ingredients that are to be cooked inside and folding the leaf over into a neat package. Often you will need a cocktail stick or thin satay stick to secure the package. Food wrapped in this way is usually broiled or sometimes steamed, the resulting food having the added flavor of the banana leaf itself. Apart from the taste, foil is an acceptable alternative. Banana leaves can also be used as plates or plate liners, as well as being made into banana cups to hold food during cooking (see page 26 for instructions).

BASIL LEAVES

There are three types of basil. Sweet basil (*bai horapha*) is used widely in curries and some stir-fry dishes. It has dark, glossy leaves with a strong, pungent flavor. Holy basil (*bai krapao*) has longer, narrower, and lighter-colored leaves. It gives off its full flavor, which is hot and spicy, much like cloves, only when cooked and is often used as an ingredient in stir-fry dishes. Finally, lemon basil (*bai mangluk*) is popular in the northeastern region of Thailand in soups and salads.

BEAN CURD

Fragile looking 3-inch squares of fresh bean curd, or tofu, are sold in the refrigerated section of oriental stores from an open box covered with fresh water. The bean curd is made from soybean milk set with gypsum. In spite of its bland flavor, it is full of protein and used throughout the whole region. It will keep in the refrigerator for three or four days if covered with fresh water daily. A long-life version is also available from supermarkets; once opened use as fresh.

Deep-fried bean curd is used in many dishes. Cubes of bean curd, which are deep-fried until golden and packaged for the freezer, are available in pouches from oriental stores. To use from the freezer, pour boiling water over them, drain after one minute, cool slightly, then squeeze the cubes to get rid of any excess oil. They can then be used whole or sliced.

BEAN SPROUTS

Used throughout the East for their appearance and texture, bean sprouts are readily available from vegetable stores and supermarkets. Choose only those sprouts that look fresh and white and have been kept in a cool place. To store, take them out of the packaging and place in a container of cold water, changing this each day. Most bean sprouts come from mung beans, though soybean sprouts are also available. Removal of the brown root and sometimes the head makes them look more attractive but can be time-consuming and unnecessary, especially if they are to be added to a stir-fry or egg rolls.

Mung beans and soybeans can both be sprouted at home. Wash mung beans well and soak overnight, then drain and rinse again. Line a deep plastic tray with a few layers of damp paper towels, sprinkle with the mung beans, and set in a warm, dark place, covering with some plastic wrap and maybe even a newspaper to make sure light is excluded. Sprinkle with water every day for six to nine days until the sprouts are fully developed. Use as soon as possible or store in the refrigerator as above. Do not grow too many at once. From 2 ounces of mung beans you get 8 ounces of sprouts. For soybeans, follow the directions on the package.

CARDAMOM

Green or white pods are readily available. Clusters of the pods grow near ground level on a plant that is a member of the ginger family. To capture the full exquisite flavor, which is warm and pungent with a hint of lemon, dry-fry if the recipe suggests it, then bruise the pods and prise them open. Remove the tiny black seeds, which can be crushed and added to a range of dishes, particularly chicken.

CHILIES

These are an indispensable ingredient. There are two main types in Thai cooking: the finger-sized chili *prik chii faa*, which comes in red or green and sometimes orange, and the tiny bird's eye, or scud, chili, *prik khee noo*, which is even more powerful and is used extensively. Chili addicts can even be seen eating these whole. Whichever type you are using, treat it with great respect: The oils from the chili must not get near your lips or eyes because they will sting. To prepare for cooking, simply remove the cap from the chili, then slit from top to bottom under running water and scoop out the seeds (unless you like your food fiercely hot). Use rubber gloves or wash your hands thoroughly with soap and water after preparation. Slice, then pound to a paste using a mortar and pestle or use a food processor.

You can buy a good quality chili paste sold under the name of *sambal ulek* (red chili). Two fresh chilies are equivalent to one teaspoon of chili paste.

Dried chilies are sold widely and are very convenient. These can be seeded, if liked, and then ground to a powder using a mortar and pestle or soaked in warm water for 15 minutes before being pounded into a paste.

Chili powder is easily obtainable when all the other alternatives cannot be found. Buy little and often, and store away from the light so that it retains its flavor and color.

CHINESE MUSHROOMS

Good quality mushrooms might seem expensive, but they do add a distinctive flavor to a variety of dishes. They must be soaked in water 20–30 minutes before being used. Remove and drain the mushrooms, discard the stems, then use the mushrooms whole or cut into slices. The soaking liquid can be used as stock or in soups.

CILANTRO

This spice is used in large quantities in all Thai cooking and is available in good vegetable stores and supermarkets. Ideally, buy a real bunch, roots and all. Keep in a plastic bag secured with a rubber band in the salad drawer in the refrigerator. The leaves are used all over Southeast Asia in salads and as a garnish, but the Thais also pound the stalks and roots to give an extra dimension to their curries, especially the renowned green variety. It has a distinctive pungent smell that complements a multitude of dishes. A cilantro stem in the recipes denotes a single-rooted plant that has several stalks. Many bunches are sadly sold without the root, so use 4–5 stems as an equivalent.

CINNAMON

You can buy cinnamon either whole in sticks or ground, which is sold loose or in jars. Cinnamon is more widely associated with sweet dishes in the West, but in the cooking of Southeast Asia its spicy fragrance is appreciated in curries.

COCONUTS

Known as *ma prow*, or food of the gods, huge plantations are nurtured to produce the phenomenal quantities of coconut milk and cream required by Thailand's cooks. There is a big business in canning, freeze-drying, and freezing the liquid for export. Coconut milk and cream can be homemade from dried coconut (unsweetened) (see opposite), although for quality and convenience canned milk cannot be faulted. If you need fresh coconut for a recipe, select one that sounds full of juice when it is shaken. (This juice is pleasant to drink, so if you wish to save it, either pierce one of the "eyes" of the coconut and drain it off or open the coconut carefully and collect the juice in a bowl.) To open a coconut, hold it in your left hand (if you are left-handed, swap the instructions). Make sure the "eyes" are just above your thumb, then, using the back of a cleaver, strike the top or crown of the coconut. The coconut will fall apart easily after two or three blows. Alternatively, place the coconut on a patio or a similar surface and hit with a hammer twice on the crown for the same effect.

Coconut juice—The liquid inside the coconut when it is shaken is coconut juice, not coconut milk. It is a refreshing drink but it is tricky to capture the juice. It is also made into palm wine, which can be quite potent.

Freshly grated coconut—When a little water is added, the coconut milk can be squeezed out by hand.

Canned coconut milk—This is available in 13½-ounce cans, which come mostly from Thailand. It is more expensive to buy this ready-prepared product, but it is much more convenient and of excellent quality.

Instant powdered coconut—Instructions on the package show how to make cream, rich milk, or milk according to how much water you add. The great advantage of using powdered coconut is that you can quickly make very small quantities as required.

Dried coconut (unsweetened)—This is a very successful and inexpensive way of making good quality coconut milk and cream, though it is labor intensive. Empty the contents of an 8-ounce package of dried coconut (unsweetened) into a food processor and pour over 1¾ cups boiling water. Process 20–30 seconds and let cool a little. If making several batches, empty each quantity into a large bowl after processing and let cool. Place a strainer lined with muslin over a large bowl. Ladle some of the coconut into the muslin and fold the edges over, then twist the ends to squeeze out the maximum amount of milk. Repeat with the remaining coconut, discarding the used coconut each time. (You can use it to make a second batch, but it will be of poorer quality and should be used only to extend a good quality first squeezing.) The coconut cream will float to the top of the milk, as cream does with cow's milk. After 10 minutes you can scoop off the cream to use in a recipe as directed. Any leftover coconut milk or cream can be stored in the refrigerator for a day, or for longer in the freezer.

Creamed coconut—This is sold in blocks, which must be kept in the refrigerator. Small slices can be added at the end of cooking curries or as instructed on the package.

CORIANDER SEEDS

These tiny, ball-shaped, beige-colored seeds disguise their potential as one of the most highly regarded spices in Thai cooking. For the full impact, dry-fry over gentle heat a few minutes, either shaking the skillet or stirring the seeds until they start to give off a spicy aroma. Grind to a fine powder and savor the heady perfume. It will discourage you from buying ready-ground coriander ever again!

CUMIN SEEDS

These scented seeds are frequently used with coriander seeds as a blend of spices. The two are used in garam masala and in many fish, chicken, and meat curries, and pastes. The seeds look something like hay seeds and should not be confused with fennel seeds, which are larger and have an aniseed flavor. Dry-fry and grind to a powder for the best results.

CURRY PASTES

There is a great deal of satisfaction to be had in making your own curry paste from scratch. You will need a considerable quantity of fresh chilies, so it is a good idea to make rubber gloves if you are making several of the pastes at once. Do remember to scrape out the seeds from the chilies under running water so that the oils don't get into your eyes, and use a food processor to make the spicy ingredients into a first-class paste using the recipes on pages 24–5 . In Thailand the pastes are often made by hand, which results in a smoother consistency, but the prepared pastes that are available from markets and some supermarkets are perfectly acceptable for taste and texture.

Make up at least the quantity given in the recipe, and store the remainder in the refrigerator in a glass jar (plastic containers retain the strong smells). Remember to write on a label how many tablespoons there are in the jar. It will keep for several weeks in the refrigerator. Alternatively, freeze two tablespoons at a time in plastic wrap, overwrapped with foil.

There are many ready-made curry pastes on the market, some of very good quality, which will cut down on the preparation time. Try out several before you find one that suits you. They are available in small pouches, jars, or large tubs, which are economical if Thai cooking has caught your imagination. The following information will help you identify the different curry pastes you might find: red curry paste (*krueng gaeng phed*), green curry paste (*gaeng khiew waan*), jungle curry paste or country style (*gaeng pah*).

EGGPLANTS

These are also known as brinjal (a name of Indian origin). There are many different types, from the long purple variety to the white/green type, about the size of a ping-pong ball, which can be eaten raw with Nam Prik Sauce (see page 50), or pounded with the ingredients for a sauce, or added to curries. The garden pea type can be used in the same way in the sauce or as an addition to a green curry.

FERMENTED HOT AND SOUR MUSTARD GREENS

Fiery and hot as the name suggests, this vegetable is drained and finely chopped for use as an accompaniment to Chiang Mai Curried Noodle Soup with Chicken (see page 70). A milder version, also sold in cans, is fermented lettuce with chili served in the same way. Either ingredient can be added to a vegetable stir-fry to add a little zip.

FISH SAUCE

Also known as *nam pla* in Thailand, fish sauce is widely used for flavoring. It is made throughout Southeast Asia, with each nationality claiming that its brand is best. Thailand exports the sauce in great quantities. It is made by packing anchovies into barrels with salt; the liquid that is eventually collected is the fish sauce. It is strong in flavor, both fishy and salty, as you would expect, and is used to accentuate and complement other flavors. It is easy to find and keeps very well in a cool place.

GARLIC

This is used all over the region in very substantial quantities. The whole garlic is called a "bulb" and each segment a "clove." Choose plump-looking bulbs and store in a cool place. Many recipes require crushed garlic and for this you can use a garlic press or a mortar and pestle. Simply trim away the root before crushing.

GINGER

Young ginger, with its pale, creamy root, delicate pink nodules, and green tips, can be bought all over Southeast Asia. It is used finely chopped in many stir-fry and fish dishes, but does not impart the pungent, aromatic flavor of the older, silvery-brown-skinned type that is readily available. Young ginger forms the basis for the exquisitely carved fish, birds, and flowers in Thai cuisine. The older type, known as a hand, must be either peeled or scraped, then sliced, and either chopped or pounded before being used.

Bruised ginger is suggested in some recipes. To bruise it, peel or scrape, then give a sharp blow with the end of a rolling pin or using a mortar and pestle. The piece will then release its juices during cooking and can be removed from the dish before serving. Wrap closely in newspaper and store in the salad drawer in the refrigerator. *See also* kha and krachai.

KAPI

An essential ingredient in the cooking of Southeast Asia, kapi is made from tiny shrimp and salt, which are allowed to ferment, then pounded into a fine paste. Dull pink to dark brown, fermented shrimp paste is generally sold in 8-ounce blocks, although the Thai variety is available in 2-ounce plastic containers. It keeps very well once opened if you rewrap it closely and store in an airtight container in a cool place. It has an unforgettable smell on first acquaintance but, strangely enough, does not dominate other flavors, but adds depth and pungency, which are so much a part of the foods of the region. Where a recipe specifies ½ inch kapi, interpret this as a cube and prepare as follows. Either mold the kapi on to the end of a skewer and rotate over a low-to-medium gas flame or under the broiler of an electric stove, until the outside begins to look crusty but not burned. Alternatively, to avoid such a strong smell, wrap the kapi in foil and place in a dry skillet over low heat 5 minutes, turning from time to time. This process takes away the rawness from the kapi and is essential when the kapi is to be included in, say, a dressing or nam prik sauce. If the kapi is to be fried with other spices, this preliminary cooking may be omitted.

KHA

This member of the ginger family can sometimes be bought fresh from oriental stores. It is creamy colored with rings on the skin, and if you are lucky enough to buy young kha it may even have pink buds. The stems are straighter than the knobbly ones of ginger. To prepare, trim off the size you require, then peel and slice before using. The flesh is much more woody and fibrous than ginger, and has a pine-like smell. It is an essential ingredient in the famous *tom yum goong*—Thailand's best loved soup (see page 73). Store wrapped in newspaper in the bottom of the refrigerator, where it will keep for two weeks or more. Dried kha powder (*laos*) can be bought; use one teaspoon for each ½ inch used in the recipe, though it is not nearly as good as the real thing.

KRACHAI

The third member of the ginger family looks like a bunch of fingers. These are sliced diagonally and added to curries such as the Jungle Curry on page 101, where they give an earthy element to the dish. Store like ginger and kapi.

LEMONGRASS

Fresh lemongrass stems are available in oriental stores, good quality vegetable stores, and some supermarkets. Huge clumps of this grass grow freely in warm climates. The long, slender leaves can be used to make a tea infusion, but the tightly packed stem, which is sometimes likened to a rather flat scallion, is used in every country of the region for its wondrous lemony aroma and flavor. To prepare, cut off the root end and discard, then trim off the lower 2½-inch piece. This is sliced and sometimes pounded according to the recipe. Even as you cut the stem, just smell the marvelous lemon aroma. The top end of the stem can be either bruised and added to a curry for extra flavor (remove before serving if you like), or it can be bruised to make a brush with which to baste the meats on satay sticks with a little oil as they cook, or to stir a sauce (see page 31). This is another illustration of the resourcefulness of Southeast Asian cooks: Nothing is discarded. See also Thai Fish Cakes on page 46 for a clever way of using lemongrass stems.

Lemongrass will keep well for two to three weeks if closely wrapped in newspaper and placed in the salad drawer of the refrigerator. For longer-term storage, prepare as directed above, then place the pounded, fleshy part in a plastic box in the freezer, making a note of how many stems have been pounded. When firm, mark into sections of, say, two stems per portion for future use. The top part of the stems can be wrapped closely and frozen too. Freeze-dried lemongrass is also available in jars from good supermarkets, which can be used instead: Use one teaspoon for each stem. Some books suggest using a strip of lemon zest, but this is no substitute for the real thing.

LIME LEAVES (MAGRUT)

Known as *bai magrut*, these leaves really catch the eye: They are dark green and glossy with a "waist." They come from the kaffir lime tree, and are used widely in Thai cuisine. They are torn or finely shredded, then added to an enormous range of dishes from soups to curries, contributing a unique lime/lemon flavor. For long-term storage, wrap washed leaves and store in the freezer. No thawing is required before use, which makes this a very convenient way of storing them. (Freeze-dried kaffir lime leaves are now available in jars from major supermarkets.) If you cannot get hold of lime leaves, use grated grapefruit zest as a substitute.

The fruit, known as the kaffir lime, or magrut, resembles a rather gnarled lemon. Only the zest is used in recipes, finely grated, though a dried variety is available. It must be soaked before use.

MANGO

Green mangoes are very popular in salads (see page 97).
To prepare a ripe mango, see page 178.

NOODLES

Egg noodles—Referred to as *bah mee*, these rich yellow
noodles are available fresh or frozen from oriental stores
and supermarkets. If not frozen, use within two days. Either
allow to thaw at room temperature or plunge into boiling
water briefly until soft, stirring often, then drain and use
as directed. Dried egg noodles are also available: Soak
10 minutes in water before cooking in salted, boiling water
2 minutes until tender, or follow the package directions.

Rice noodles—Known as *guay tiew*, these can be bought
fresh from some oriental stores. The wide strips, which are
folded sometimes and look like cannelloni, contain flecks
of dried shrimp or scallions. Plunge into boiling water. Drain,
then cut the still-folded noodles into narrow strips and use in
stir-fries. Keep covered before cooking to prevent the noodles
drying out.

Flat dried rice noodles—These come in three widths
and are referred to as *sen mei* (⅛ inch), *sen lek* (¼ inch), and *sen yai*
(⅜ inch). Soak in warm water 15 minutes if required quickly
or place in cold water and leave until you are ready to cook.
Drain and use in stir-fries or soups.

Rice vermicelli—These very thin round noodles are
deep-fried for *mee krob* (see page 149) or soaked in warm
water 1–2 minutes before being drained and then used in
soups or stir-fry recipes.

Bean thread noodles—These are made from mung
beans and they resemble nylon fishing line gathered up into
a skein. Soak them in warm water 10 minutes before draining
and cutting them into short lengths with scissors. Use in
appetizers such as Thai Egg Rolls (see page 42) and Money
Bags (see page 54) or add to soups.

OYSTER SAUCE

Made from an extract of oysters, soy sauce, salt, and starches,
oyster sauce gives a characteristic flavor to meat dishes and
vegetables in particular. It keeps well, but you may need to
add a little boiling water if it thickens up as you reach the end
of the bottle.

PANDANUS LEAF

This resembles a gladiolius leaf, and is a very popular addition
to rice dishes and desserts, to which it imparts a warm flavor.
It is also wonderful in plain boiled or steamed rice. For the
maximum flavor, hold the leaf at one end and pull the prongs
of a fork through it, then tie it in a knot and add to the recipe
as directed (see Coconut Rice on page 30). It is available fresh
from oriental stores; keep any extra leaves in the freezer.

PEANUTS OR GROUNDNUTS

The alternative name for these nuts is apt, because they have to be dug from the ground at harvest time. In many countries this is done by hand. The nuts are highly nutritious, with a 30 percent protein content and a 40–50 percent oil content. They are used widely all over the region in many dishes, sauces, and for garnishing. If salted peanuts are used instead, remember to taste before adding extra salt. Crunchy peanut butter is an alternative to crushed and pounded peanuts in the sauces in this book. Peanut or groundnut oil is popular for cooking and widely available. Roast raw peanuts in a wok without oil, turning, about 8 minutes until golden. Cool and store.

PEPPERCORNS

These grow on a vine, which is trained up a tripod shaped structure. The berries grow in clusters like tiny grapes, are harvested when ripe, and then dried in the sun on large mats, where they are turned regularly and become black peppercorns. For white peppercorns, the berries are soaked in running water for a week to rot the hard casing, then rubbed by hand to remove this completely before being sun-dried.

PORK CRACKLING

Also known as *chicaron*, this is made from pork rind that has been deep-fried, forming puffy, crisp crackers. It is sold in oriental stores and is served as the crunchy element alongside curries, sliced in salads, or with Nam Prik Sauce (see page 50).

PRESERVED PLUMS

These add a sharp, salty taste (see the sauce on page 154). They are sold in jars, and any leftovers will keep in the refrigerator. Do not discard the clear liquid.

RICE

This is a staple food for two-thirds of the world's population. Thai fragrant long-grain rice is widely available and has a high reputation for both quality and perfume. Many homes in which rice is consumed in large quantities have a rice cooker (see page 21).

RICE WINE VINEGAR

This is a mild vinegar. You could use white wine or cider vinegar instead.

SESAME SEEDS

After India and China, Burma is the third largest producer of sesame seeds. The whole plant is cut at harvest time and stacked upright until the seed pods begin to burst open, releasing the tiny seeds. The seeds are widely used in oriental cooking, either dry-fried or toasted to extract their delicious nutty flavor. Two other products come from the seeds: tahini, which is a crushed sesame paste, and sesame oil. The seeds are rich in oil (45–50 percent). The oil is not used for frying since it has a low burning temperature, but it is often used to dress vegetables just before serving.

SHALLOTS

These mild members of the onion family are widely used, but if you cannot buy them, substitute one red onion for six to eight shallot segments. (This will give a much deeper color to your finished dish.) Alternatively, use a brown-skinned Spanish-type onion.

SHRIMP

The dried varieties are sun-dried and therefore have a long shelf life. They are usually sold in packages and need to be soaked in water and drained before being used whole or chopped in soups or with vegetables. In some recipes the dried shrimp are pounded to make a powder using a mortar and pestle or food processor. Make up a quantity if making many Thai dishes. Powdered shrimp are also sold in packages.

SHRIMP CHIPS

These have become universally popular not only as an accompaniment to Southeast Asian food but also as a cocktail snack. They are sold in 8-ounce bags, which should be stored in a cool, dry place. To cook, follow the instructions on page 53. Leftovers (in the rare cases that there are any) can be stored in an airtight container.

SOY SAUCE

This is an indispensable ingredient in the cooking of Southeast Asia. Each country uses a light (thin) and a dark (thick) soy sauce. The sauce is made from fermented soybeans, wheat grain, salt, and water. Light soy sauce is the most widely used. Dark, or thick, soy sauce is, as the name suggests, much thicker and darker in color, so add with care. It also has a sugar content, unlike the light (thin) sauce. Mushroom-flavored dark soy sauce imparts a lot of depth in flavoring.

SQUID

Ready-cleaned squid can be easily bought either fresh or frozen from larger supermarkets. If frozen, thaw, then pull the tentacles from each pocket when sufficiently thawed. Slit down the side of the pocket and open it out. Score the inner surface lightly with the back of a knife and cut each one into two or three strips. They will curl obligingly in the hot wok, as will the tentacles, and the scoring helps the sauce to permeate the flesh. These curls look so pretty, but you can save time by simply cutting the squid into rings.

STRAW MUSHROOMS

Sold in cans, these are an attractive addition to many vegetable, fish, and stir-fry recipes. They are grown in straw, as the name suggests. Button mushrooms are an acceptable alternative.

STOCK

A really good fish or chicken stock will enhance the flavor of all your recipes (see page 23 for recipes), though you can use stock cubes and water if necessary. Make the stock using fish bones, shrimp shells, a chicken carcass, or a pack of chicken wings. I often buy a whole chicken when just needing the leg and breast meat for a recipe and then use the carcass to make stock to store in the freezer in 1½ cup quantities. Remember to label before freezing, since all stocks look the same when they come out of the freezer.

If you have square plastic boxes (a good shape for storing in the freezer), stick a label on a plastic bag and place it in a box, then fill. When the stock is frozen, you can remove the stock in the bag from the box and tie up the top. Return to the freezer until required. The box is now free for other uses.

TAMARIND

This is used to add tartness to recipes all over the region, just as we might use vinegar or lemon juice. The tamarind tree produces large pods about the size of a lima bean. They are sometimes sold loose, but the more usual way is to buy the puree from the pod in an 8-ounce block, which looks rather like a block of dates. It keeps for a long time if closely wrapped in a cool place.

To make tamarind juice, mix one teaspoon of tamarind pulp with a few tablespoons of warm water. Let stand 10 minutes, then mix by hand to release the pulp from the seeds. Strain, then discard the pulp and seeds; the resulting tamarind water is ready to be used in a recipe. Tamarind puree makes this even easier: use one tablespoon to four tablespoons of water. A ready-made juice is also available.

Dried tamarind looks something like dried apple slices. It also needs to be soaked (use two slices in water just to cover), but because it is dry you need to allow 30 minutes to extract the maximum flavor, then strain and use the juice.

WATER CHESTNUTS

Canned water chestnuts are added to dishes for their crisp, crunchy texture. Any leftovers can be added to a fruit salad or used in Thai Rubies in Sweetened Coconut Milk (see page 186).

WING BEANS

These unusual-looking light green beans have a type of frill down four sides. This attractive feature is shown to advantage when the beans are sliced diagonally before cooking. Choose the smaller ones for crispness—they are tougher when older. Use them in stir-fries (see page 121) and salads or blanch before serving with Nam Prik Sauce (see page 50). If unavailable, use string beans instead.

WRAPPERS

Egg roll and wonton wrappers come in square and round shapes and in different sizes. They are usually to be found in the freezer section of an oriental store. Allow them to thaw then, when ready for use, open the pack and very carefully tease up one corner from the pile and peel away. Repeat this until all the wrappers have been placed in a separate pile. Cover with a slightly damp cloth to prevent drying out before filling.

EQUIPMENT

BARBECUE

Some recipes, such as the barbecue ones included in this book, or satay dishes, gain extra flavor by being cooked over charcoal. A gas or electric broiler can be used, but charcoal does add to the flavor, and is essential if you want to cook and eat a Thai meal outdoors.

CLEAVER

This multipurpose, heavy, broad-bladed implement is used with great skill by oriental cooks for chopping, slicing, and grinding, or even crushing a peeled clove of garlic by simply pressing down on the broad side of the blade.

MORTAR AND PESTLE/FOOD PROCESSOR

The mortar and pestle and/or food processor feature a great deal in the making of spice pastes and the pounding and blending of ingredients.

The traditional granite mortar and pestle is quite deep and is pitted, making it ideal for grinding and pounding wet spices. Chili, garlic, kha, ginger, and lemongrass are held by the rough surface and do not fly out while being pounded, though the ingredients should be sliced before pounding for the best results. For grinding or pounding small quantities of wet or dry spices, this type of mortar and pestle is ideal.

If using a food processor, slice fibrous ingredients such as kha, ginger, and lemongrass before processing and, if a particularly fine, smooth paste is required, bruise them first using the mortar and pestle. If you add oil to the spice paste ingredients to ease the blending, do remember to reduce the amount of oil for frying the paste to compensate for this.

RICE COOKER

If you eat a lot of rice and want a foolproof method of achieving perfect results every time, plus rice that is kept warm until you need it, then a rice cooker is a sensible choice.

STEAMERS

Bamboo, stacking-type steamers are available in a host of sizes from a wide range of stores. They are multipurpose in that they can be used for serving as well as cooking the food.

WOK

This wide, circular pan with a curved base not only enables you to cook a large quantity of food simultaneously over a large surface but also allows for the rapid evaporation of liquid, which is essential in many recipes. It is the ideal shape for tossing food in stir-fry recipes, is a much more satisfactory shape than a skillet for deep-frying, and can also be used for steaming. Buy the heaviest one you can find, since the very thin, lightweight woks will burn food very easily. If you have a gas stove, you will need to use a metal stand for the wok.

A useful tip: Warm the wok over gentle heat before adding the oil, which will flood over the heated surface more easily and prevent food from sticking.

COOKING METHODS

BARBECUING

Charcoal is used extensively for cooking throughout Southeast Asia. Where this is not feasible, use the broiler for satay, for example, or roast in the oven if portions of spareribs or chicken are used in a recipe (see pages 166 and 169).

DEEP-FRYING

The wok is ideal for deep-frying, requiring less oil than conventional deep-frying saucepans yet providing a larger surface area for cooking. Use a thermometer to keep an eye on the temperature, if possible.

STEAMING

The beauty of bamboo baskets stacked neatly on top of each other is that they give great versatility: You can use just one basket or several over the same wok. Do not fill the baskets too full, or the steam will not penetrate evenly. Aluminum Chinese-style steamers are sold in Chinese stores and usually consist of two perforated trays with a lid to sit above a saucepan. When steaming, always have a kettle of boiling water ready to fill up the wok, steamer base, or saucepan. The Thais like to use banana leaf packages for steaming whole fish in particular (see Steamed Whole Fish with Preserved Plums in Banana Leaf Package on page 154).

When small items are being cooked, line each basket with a piece of damp muslin. You can then stack them one on top of the other with the lid set on top before setting them over the wok, replenishing the boiling water as necessary. If you have a metal trivet that sits in the wok over the water, you can cook, say, a whole fish in a large dish. Cover with a lid and keep an eye on the water level while it is steaming.

Finally, a two-tier electric steamer is a real boon when the top of the stove is being used for curries and stir-fry dishes and there is no space for a steamer.

STIR-FRYING

No matter what is being cooked, all the ingredients for a stir-fry must be ready before you start cooking, since the whole process is essentially fast in order to retain maximum flavor, color, and crispness, especially when cooking vegetables.

When all the ingredients are ready, warm the wok over gentle heat, then pour in the oil and swirl it around before adding the first ingredients, be it spice paste or chopped onion, garlic, or ginger. (You will need considerably less oil for stir-frying than for conventional frying, which is a plus point from the health point of view.) When stir-frying, you must keep everything on the move all the time to insure even cooking. The reason for adding ingredients at high temperatures is to seal in the juices of the finely chopped ingredients, so retaining all the flavor. Some vegetables, such as broccoli, should be quickly plunged into boiling water (this is known as blanching), then drained and rinsed with cold water to retain their bright green color, before being added to the stir-fry dish.

STOCKS

FISH OR CHICKEN STOCK
NAHM SUP GOONG OR *NAHM SUP GAI*

MAKES **4 CUPS**   PREPARATION TIME: **10** MINUTES
COOKING TIME: **35** MINUTES

1 pound **fish bones** from sole, cod, or other white fish,
  or 1 **chicken** carcass, broken into pieces, or 1 pack
  chicken wings
1 **onion**, quartered
1-inch piece fresh **ginger**, bruised
1 **lemongrass** stem, bruised
1 **lime leaf** (optional)
6 **cilantro** stems, stalks and roots bruised (optional)
salt and freshly ground **black pepper**

1 **WASH** the fish or raw chicken bones in cold water first.
  Place in a large saucepan and cover with 6 cups water.
2 **BRING** to a boil, then skim if necessary.
3 **ADD** the onion, ginger, lemongrass, lime leaf, and cilantro,
  if using, and some seasoning. Return to a boil, turn the heat
  down, and then simmer 20 minutes only, without a lid, for
  the fish stock or 30 minutes (half-covered) for the chicken
  stock. Remove from the heat.
4 **COOL**, then strain into a clean container. Use immediately,
  or cool and chill, or freeze in small quantities until required.

VEGETABLE STOCK
NAHM SUP PAK

MAKES **6 CUPS**   PREPARATION TIME: **10** MINUTES
COOKING TIME: **30—40** MINUTES

1½ pounds (total weight) of the following **vegetables**:
  white cabbage, carrots, celery, leeks, and onions
8 cups **water**
1 teaspoon **salt** and a little freshly ground **black pepper**
4 teaspoons **light soy sauce**
½ teaspoon **sugar**

1 **DISCARD** the outer leaves and the thick stalks from
  the piece of cabbage and shred finely. Chop the carrots,
  chop the celery stalks, slice the leeks, and cut the onions
  into quarters.
2 **PLACE** the prepared vegetables and water in a large
  saucepan. Add the salt and pepper and bring to a boil.
  Reduce the heat, half-cover, and simmer 30—40 minutes
  until the vegetables are tender.
3 **STRAIN** the stock through a fine strainer and return it to
  the saucepan.
4 **BOIL** a further 5 minutes without a lid. Stir in the soy
  sauce and sugar.
5 **COOL**, then use immediately or cool completely and chill,
  or freeze in small quantities until required.

PASTES

RED CURRY PASTE

KRUENG GAENG PHED

MAKES 1½ CUPS   PREPARATION TIME: 30–35 MINUTES
COOKING TIME: 2–3 MINUTES

10 **red chilies**, seeded and sliced

¼ pound **red onions** or **shallots**, sliced

4 **garlic** cloves, sliced

3 **lemongrass** stems, lower stem only, sliced and bruised

½-inch piece **kha**, peeled and sliced

4 **cilantro** stems, stalks and roots only

1–2 tablespoons **sunflower oil**

1 teaspoon grated **magrut**

½-inch cube prepared **kapi** (*see page 15*)

1 tablespoon **coriander seeds**

2 teaspoons **cumin seeds**

8–10 **black peppercorns**

1 teaspoon **salt**

1 **BLEND** the chilies, onions or shallots, garlic, lemongrass, kha, and cilantro to a fine paste with the oil in a food processor. Add the magrut and prepared kapi.

2 **DRY-FRY** the seeds for a few minutes, then grind to a powder with the peppercorns using a mortar and pestle. Add to the paste with the salt. Blend well. Spoon into a glass jar, cover with plastic wrap and a tight-fitting lid, and refrigerate.

GREEN CURRY PASTE

GAENG KHIEW WAAN

MAKES 1⅓ CUPS   PREPARATION TIME: 30–35 MINUTES
COOKING TIME: 2–3 MINUTES

10 **green chilies**, seeded and sliced

¼ pound **white onions** or **shallots**, sliced

4 **garlic** cloves, sliced

3 **lemongrass** stems, lower stem only, sliced and bruised

½-inch piece **kha**, peeled and sliced

4 **cilantro** stems, leaves, stalks, and roots

4 **lime leaves**, sliced

1–2 tablespoons **sunflower oil**

1 teaspoon grated **magrut**

½-inch cube prepared **kapi** (*see page 15*)

1 tablespoon **coriander seeds**

2 teaspoons **cumin seeds**

8–10 **black peppercorns**

1 teaspoon **salt**

1 **BLEND** the chilies, onions or shallots, garlic, lemongrass, kha, cilantro, and lime leaves to a fine paste with the oil in a food processor. Add the magrut and prepared kapi.

2 **DRY-FRY** the seeds for a few minutes, then grind to a powder with the peppercorns using a mortar and pestle. Add to the spice paste with the salt. Store as for red curry paste.

MUSSAMAN CURRY PASTE

GAENG MUSSAMAN

MAKES 1¼ CUPS   PREPARATION TIME: 30–35 MINUTES
COOKING TIME: 5 MINUTES

Assemble and prepare the same ingredients as for the red curry paste, but follow the different preparation of the fresh ingredients. The frying greatly enhances the flavors before the mixture is processed into a paste.

red curry paste ingredients (*see page 24*)

6 **cardamom pods**

½ teaspoon **ground cloves**

½ teaspoon **cinnamon**

1 FRY the chilies with the onions, garlic, lemongrass, and kha in a little oil, stirring 3 minutes over low heat to bring out the flavors.

2 PLACE in a food processor and blend the ingredients to a smooth paste. Add the cilantro stalks, magrut, and kapi. Blend again.

3 FRY the coriander and cumin seeds in a dry skillet a few minutes with the cardamom pods and salt. Remove the seeds from the pods and pound to a powder with the black peppercorns using a mortar and pestle.

4 ADD the cloves and cinnamon, put into a food processor with the spice paste, and blend again until very smooth.

HUNG LAY CURRY PASTE

GAENG HUNG LAY

MAKES 1 CUP   PREPARATION TIME: 25 MINUTES

1-inch cube prepared **kapi** (*see page 15*)

10 **dried red chilies**, some or all of the seeds removed, torn into pieces

1 ounce **kha**, thinly peeled and sliced

2 **lemongrass** stems, lower 2½ inches trimmed and sliced, stems bruised

3 **garlic** cloves

3 large **shallots**, halved

1 PUT all the ingredients into a food processor and process until the paste is well blended.

2 TRANSFER to a screwtop glass jar with some plastic wrap between the jar and lid. Refrigerate for up to 2 months.

GARNISHES

BANANA CUPS

1 PLACE a banana leaf on a large chopping board. Mark out disks using a 5½-inch saucer for the smaller size cups or a 7-inch plate to match the larger ramekins.

2 CUT around the disks with a sharp knife and plunge into a bowl of boiling water.

3 PLACE two leaf disks together with the undersides facing and with the grain of each going in a different direction, which strengthens the cup shape.

4 MAKE a tuck at one point and staple firmly. Repeat with the opposite side and then at the other two corners to obtain a cup shape. These are shown with Khun Nan's Steamed Fish Curry on page 113.

CHILI FLOWERS

1 CHOOSE a small, finger-long chili and slit the top two-thirds of it into fine strips.

2 LEAVE it in cold, or even ice, water to speed up the curling operation, then scrape away the seeds, if wished.

CUCUMBER GARNISHES

1 MAKE a fan by cutting notches down each side of the skin of a 3-inch piece of cucumber then slicing thinly toward the end without cutting right through.

2 MAKE a folded garnish by thinly slicing a 6-inch piece of cucumber almost through to the bottom, then folding it in alternate slices. (Thai cucumbers are fairly pliable.)

SCALLION CURLS

1 CHOOSE a finger-long piece of scallion, firm green part only, and discard the root.

2 HOLD it in the center and use a sharp knife to cut the stem into strips from the center to the end in each direction.

3 PLACE in cold water to curl.

4 CREATE a variation by threading a slice of chili on to the finger-long piece of stem in the middle and repeating the cutting as above.

SCALLION TASSELS

1 CHOOSE the white root part of a not-too-large scallion that has a little green top to it.

2 CUT it to finger length and discard the root. Hold at the base and, using a sharp knife, cut the top two-thirds through and up to the top several times.

3 PLACE in cold water to curl. This makes a very attractive garnish for the center of a dish.

SAUCES

DIPPING SAUCES

MAKES A GENEROUS 2 CUPS   PREPARATION TIME: 3–4 MINUTES
COOKING TIME: 8–9 MINUTES

The basic dipping sauce has a sugar syrup base with the addition of vinegar and salt. This underlines the three basic flavors in Thai food: sweet, sour, and salty.

2 cups **sugar**

2 cups **water**

2 tablespoons **wine vinegar** or **rice vinegar**

1½ tablespoons **salt**

1 HEAT the sugar and water together in a saucepan, stirring until the sugar dissolves. Let boil 4–5 minutes to become syrupy. Remove from the heat and add the vinegar and salt.

2 RETURN to the heat and boil 2 minutes, then remove from the heat and cool. Divide as suggested below.

3 POUR half the prepared sugar syrup into a separate pan, and use this for the sweet chili dipping sauce (see right).

4 DIVIDE the remaining syrup between two saucepans, and use these to make the preserved plum dipping sauce and dark soy dipping sauce (see right).

5 ADD each flavoring, then return to a boil, turn the heat down, and simmer a further 1 minute.

6 COOL and transfer to glass jars. If the syrup thickens too much, add a little boiling water and stir. Cover each jar with plastic wrap, then seal with a lid.

Sweet Chili Dipping Sauce   *NAM PRIK WAAN*

Add 6 tablespoons sweet chili sauce to 1¼ cups prepared sugar syrup.

Preserved Plum Dipping Sauce   *NAM BOUY*

Add 3–4 finely chopped preserved plums to ½ cup prepared sugar syrup.

Dark Soy Dipping Sauce   *SI-EW WAAN*

Add 1 tablespoon dark soy sauce to ½ cup prepared sugar syrup.

PEANUT SAUCE *NAM JEEM SATAY*

MAKES **2** CUPS   PREPARATION TIME: **15** MINUTES
COOKING TIME: **8–10** MINUTES

*Delicious morsels of barbecued meats or shrimp on bamboo or
wooden skewers are complemented by this famous peanut sauce.*

2 teaspoons **tamarind pulp**

1⅔ cups canned **coconut milk**

1–2 teaspoons **Mussaman curry paste** (*see page 25*)

2 tablespoons **dark brown sugar**

1–2 teaspoons **fish sauce**

½–¾ cup **roasted peanuts**, coarsely ground,
   or **crunchy peanut butter**

1 SOAK the tamarind pulp in 2 tablespoons warm water
   10 minutes, then strain (see page 20). Meanwhile, pour
   one-third of the coconut milk into a wok or saucepan
   and heat through until bubbling.

2 ADD the curry paste and cook gently 2–3 minutes, stirring
   all the time to bring out the full flavor.

3 ADD the sugar, remaining coconut milk, strained
   tamarind, and fish sauce to taste. Allow to bubble to thicken
   the mixture slightly, then add the peanuts or peanut butter.

4 CONTINUE cooking, stirring, a few minutes until the
   sauce has a creamy consistency. Taste and adjust the
   seasoning by adding more fish sauce if necessary.

THAI RELISH

MAKES ½ CUP   PREPARATION TIME: **8** MINUTES

Serve this relish with a variety of snacks and appetizers.

1–2 **red chilies**, seeded and finely sliced

1-inch piece **cucumber**, halved, seeded, and finely chopped

1 **cilantro** stem

1 **shallot** or ½ small **red onion**, very finely sliced

3 tablespoons **basic dipping sauce** or **sweet chili
   dipping sauce** (*see page 27*)

1 PLACE the chilies, cucumber, chopped stalk of the
   cilantro, shallot or red onion, and dipping sauce in a
   serving bowl.

2 USE a little chili and the cilantro leaves, lightly chopped,
   for a garnish.

ALTERNATIVE TO USING DIPPING SAUCE:

1 tablespoon **sugar**

2 tablespoons **cider vinegar**

1 teaspoon **fish sauce**

1 STIR the sugar and vinegar together until the sugar has
   dissolved. Just before serving, pour this sauce over the
   chopped ingredients. Taste for seasoning and add fish sauce
   as required.

2 GARNISH as before.

BASIC RECIPES

PLAIN BOILED RICE

KHAO TOM

SERVES 4   PREPARATION TIME: 2 MINUTES
COOKING TIME: 12–15 MINUTES

1 **WASH** 1 cup rice thoroughly in several changes of water until the water looks clear to remove the starch.

2 **PLACE** the rice in a heavy-based saucepan with a generous 2 cups water and bring to a boil. Reduce the heat, stir, cover the pan, and simmer 12–15 minutes.

3 **REMOVE** the lid and stir with a chopstick or fork.

4 **USE** at once or transfer to a serving bowl, three-quarters covered with plastic wrap, and microwave on full power 4 minutes in 650w microwave or 3 minutes in 900w just before serving. Alternatively, place in an oiled steamer, cover with a lid, and set over a saucepan of gently bubbling water 8–10 minutes until well heated through. Stir with a chopstick to prevent breaking up the grains.

MICROWAVED RICE

SERVES 4   PREPARATION TIME: 2 MINUTES
COOKING TIME: 12–15 MINUTES

1 **WASH** 1 cup rice thoroughly as for boiled rice.

2 **COOK** the rice in 1¾ cups boiling water in a large bowl three-quarters covered with plastic wrap 10 minutes on full power, then rest 5 minutes in the microwave. (For easy-cook rice, follow directions on pack.)

3 **REMOVE** and stir as for boiled rice.

GLUTINOUS RICE

KHAO NIAW

SERVES 4   OVERNIGHT SOAKING TIME   COOKING TIME: 25 MINUTES

Available in black and white, this rice is very starchy, hence the common name "sticky rice." It can be gathered up into a ball with the fingers, then dipped into curries and other dishes. All over Thailand the white variety is cooked with coconut milk and served with fresh mango slices (see page 174).

1 **SOAK** 1 cup glutinous rice overnight in water to cover, then drain and rinse.

2 **PLACE** in a muslin-lined colander or steamer and place over gently bubbling water about 25 minutes (the longer the soaking, the shorter the cooking).

3 **TASTE** to check whether the rice is cooked: It should be just tender with a little resistance.

STEAMED RICE *KHAO SUAY*

SERVES 3–4   PREPARATION TIME: 3 MINUTES
COOKING TIME: 25 MINUTES

1 cup **Thai fragrant rice**

2½ cups **water**

½ teaspoon **salt**

oil for brushing

1 **PLACE** the rice in a strainer or bowl and rinse thoroughly.

2 **BOIL** the water and salt in a heavy-based saucepan. Stir in the rice.

3 **RETURN** to a boil and stir once or twice to prevent the rice settling on the saucepan bottom. Cook uncovered over medium heat until the water has been absorbed, about 6–8 minutes, and the surface is covered in tiny crater-like holes.

4 **BRUSH** the base of a steamer lightly with oil. If it has large holes, cover with either a muslin cloth or some foil that has been punctured with several holes to allow the steam to cook the rice. Drain the rice in a strainer or colander.

5 **TRANSFER** the rice into the steamer; make a few holes in the rice with a chopstick so that the steam can circulate. Set the steamer over a saucepan of boiling water. Cover with the lid and let cook 15 minutes, when the rice will be fluffy and ready to serve. Top up with boiling water as needed.

6 **FORK** through with a roasting fork or chopstick. The rice can be cooked an hour or more ahead of the meal and reheated like boiled rice (see page 29).

COCONUT RICE *HUNG KHAO MAN*

SERVES 3–4   PREPARATION TIME: 2 MINUTES
COOKING TIME: 20 MINUTES

This is a favorite accompaniment for market salad (see page 94). If you live near a Thai store, look out for fresh pandanus leaves that add a really special flavor.

1 cup **Thai fragrant rice**

scant 1 cup **coconut milk**

½ cup **water**

1 prepared **pandanus leaf** *(see page 17)*

½ teaspoon **salt**

1 tablespoon **sugar**

1 **WASH** the rice thoroughly in several changes of cold water.

2 **PLACE** the coconut milk and water in a heavy-based saucepan, first rinsed with water, and bring to a boil. Add the rice, pandanus leaf, salt, and sugar and return to a boil.

3 **REDUCE** the heat, cover with a lid, and cook gently 15 minutes, or until the rice is tender.

4 **LEAVE** in the covered saucepan a further 5 minutes before serving. Fork through with a roasting fork so that the grains remain whole and separate.

5 **REMOVE** the pandanus leaf before serving.

RICE SALAD *KHAO YUM*

SERVES **4**, OR MORE AS SIDE DISH   PREPARATION TIME: **25** MINUTES

A typically Southern Thai creation of fragrant rice piled in the center of a large serving dish, surrounded by neat piles of beautifully prepared raw vegetables, spices, and peanuts, then topped with a drizzle of fresh chili and lemon or lime juice dressing. It's a marvelous way to use up left-over rice as a quick lunch dish. You can prepare it ahead of time, putting the salad ingredients into covered containers in the refrigerator until required.

¼ pound **long** or **string beans**, cut into 1-inch lengths

3 **lemongrass** stems, lower 2½ inches removed and shredded, tops bruised

3 **carrots**, coarsely grated

⅓ pound firm **white cabbage**, very finely sliced or grated

1 bunch **scallions**, very finely shredded

2–3 **lime leaves**, finely shredded

2-inch piece fresh **ginger**, peeled and cut into matchsticks

generous 1 cup **bean sprouts**

¾ cup **roasted peanuts**

1 cup **Thai fragrant rice**, cooked and left to go cold

1 handful **sweet basil** and **cilantro leaves** to garnish

DRESSING:

3–4 **red chilies**

juice of 2 **lemons** or **limes**

3–4 tablespoons **fish sauce**

1 teaspoon **sugar**

1 **PLUNGE** the beans into boiling water then drain them, rinse with cold water, and drain again. (This process, called blanching, turns the beans a bright shade of green.)

2 **ARRANGE** all the ingredients in neat piles on one or two large serving dishes with the rice in the center not too long before the salad is to be eaten.

3 **GARNISH** the salad attractively with the basil and cilantro leaves.

4 **MAKE** the dressing. Pound the chilies using a mortar and pestle, with or without the seeds depending on how hot you like your food. (If unsure, err on the side of caution: You can always add some seeds later, but you can't take them away.)

5 **ADD** the lemon or lime juice and fish sauce little by little, tasting as you go, until it suits your taste, adding some sugar if necessary to balance the flavors. Pour into a gravy boat and stir with the bruised lemongrass stems.

6 **PLACE** the dish of rice salad in the center of the table with the gravy boat to one side. Serve, with guests taking a little of each ingredient and drizzling some of the dressing on top. Each person then tosses their salad together lightly before eating.

THAI FRIED RICE

KHAO PAD

SERVES 4   PREPARATION TIME: 20 MINUTES
COOKING TIME: 8–10 MINUTES

A stunning blend of Thai fragrant rice, cooked chicken or pork, shrimp, and vegetables, pepped-up with red curry paste, sensitively seasoned and garnished with omelet strips and lemon or lime wedges. Like Thai fried noodles, this is almost a meal in itself and takes no time to put together if the rice is already cooked and cold.

5⅓ cups cold cooked **Thai fragrant rice** (1½ cups dry weight)

4 tablespoons **sunflower oil**

2 **eggs**, beaten with 2 tablespoons **water**, lightly seasoned

1 tablespoon **red curry paste** (*see page 24*)

6 ounces **chicken** breast or boneless **pork**, very thinly sliced

1 **onion**, finely sliced

1 handful **string beans**, trimmed into short lengths

scant 1 cup canned **corn**, drained

1 tablespoon **fish sauce**

1 teaspoon **sugar**

6 ounces shelled cooked **shrimp**

4 **scallions**, trimmed and shredded

1 small handful **cilantro leaves** to garnish

1 **lemon** or **lime**, cut into fine wedges to serve

1 **STIR** the cooked rice with chopsticks or the prongs of a roasting fork to loosen the grains.

2 **HEAT** 1 tablespoon of the oil in a skillet and make two thin omelets from the egg mixture. Cook on one side only, then roll up tightly. When cold, cut into slices.

3 **HEAT** a wok and add the remaining oil. Add the curry paste, then add the chicken or pork slices, and toss all the time until they change color and are tender.

4 **ADD** the onion slices, then the beans, and continue cooking over fairly high heat, tossing all the time.

5 **ADD** the corn, rice, fish sauce, sugar, shrimp, and some of the scallions. Taste for seasoning. When very hot, place on a hot serving dish or serve from the wok.

6 **GARNISH** with the omelet slices, remaining scallions, and cilantro leaves, and serve with lemon or lime wedges.

THAI FRIED NOODLES

KUAY TIAW PAD THAI

SERVES 4–5   PREPARATION TIME: 20–25 MINUTES
COOKING TIME: 12 MINUTES

1 pound **flat dried rice noodles**

1 teaspoon **tamarind pulp**

4–5 tablespoons **sunflower oil**

2 **eggs**, beaten with 2 tablespoons **water**

salt and freshly ground **black pepper**

3 **shallots** or 1 **red onion**, roughly chopped

2 **garlic** cloves

2 **dried chilies**, seeded if liked

¼ pound **fresh bean curd**, cut into cubes (optional)

1 tablespoon **dark brown sugar**

1–2 tablespoons **fish sauce**

½ pound shelled cooked **shrimp**

2 cups **bean sprouts**

2 tablespoons **dried powdered shrimp**

scant ¼ cup **peanuts**, crushed

6 cubes **deep-fried bean curd**

1 **red chili**, seeded and shredded to garnish

1 small handful **cilantro leaves** to garnish

½ bunch **scallions**, shredded to garnish

1 **lime** or **lemon**, cut into wedges to serve

1 **COVER** the noodles with warm water to soften about 10 minutes before needed. Drain and cover with a damp cloth.

2 **SOAK** the tamarind pulp in 2 tablespoons warm water 10 minutes, then strain (see page 20).

3 **HEAT** a skillet and add 2 tablespoons of the oil. Season the beaten eggs and make two very thin omelets, cooking on one side only. Roll one into a sausage shape and cut into thin slices when cold. Leave the other whole.

4 **POUND** the shallots or red onion, garlic, and dried chilies to a paste using a mortar and pestle or food processor. Heat the remaining oil in a wok and fry the paste without browning. Add the fresh bean curd cubes, if using. Stir in the brown sugar, tamarind juice, and fish sauce to taste.

5 **ADD** the softened noodles and toss well, adding a little water if necessary to keep the noodles moist. Add the shrimp and cook over high heat 1 minute.

6 **ADD** the omelet strips and most of the bean sprouts, remove from the heat, and adjust the seasoning if necessary.

7 **PILE** the savory noodles on to a hot serving dish and sprinkle with the powdered shrimp and crushed peanuts.

8 **PLACE** the deep-fried bean curd squares in a bowl and pour boiling water over. Leave 1 minute, then drain and slice.

9 **ARRANGE** the deep-fried bean curd slices around the edge of the serving dish with the remaining bean sprouts and top with the lacy omelet. Complete the garnish with chili, cilantro leaves, and scallions, and serve with lime or lemon wedges.

SOFT-BOILED EGG NOODLES WITH PORK, CHICKEN, OR SHRIMP

BAH-MEE HAENG MOO, GAI OR GOONG

Golden egg noodles tossed with pork, chicken, or shrimp in garlic-flavored oil with bean sprouts and scallions, moistened with fish sauce and garnished with dried powdered shrimp and plenty of cilantro. Dried noodles should be soaked 10 minutes before being cooked. If using fresh noodles, shake lightly to untangle before use.

SERVES **4**   PREPARATION TIME: **12** MINUTES
COOKING TIME: **15** MINUTES

½ pound **fresh** or **dried egg noodles**

6 ounces boneless **pork** or **chicken** breast, thinly sliced,
  or same weight shelled cooked **shrimp**

2 tablespoons **sunflower oil**

1 **garlic** clove, crushed

generous 2 cups **bean sprouts**

3 **scallions,** finely shredded

1 tablespoon **fish sauce**

1 teaspoon **sugar**

salt and freshly ground **black pepper**

1 teaspoon **dried powdered shrimp** (optional)

1 handful **cilantro leaves** to garnish

1 recipe quantity **sweet chili dipping sauce**
  (*see page 27*) **to serve**

1 **SOAK** the dried noodles, if using, in warm water 10 minutes, then drain.

2 **BRING** 2½ cups water to a boil in a shallow skillet, add the pork or chicken slices, return to a boil, turn the heat down, then simmer 5–8 minutes, or until the meat slices are tender.

3 **LIFT** out the meat with a slotted spoon and reserve in a large bowl. Spoon out 6 tablespoons of the cooking liquid and reserve. If using shrimp, use stock or water instead of the cooking liquid.

4 **BRING** plenty of salted water to a boil in a large saucepan, add the fresh or drained dried noodles, and cook, stirring frequently, 2–3 minutes. Drain, rinse with hot water, and drain again. Add to the pork, chicken, or shrimp.

5 **HEAT** a wok, add the oil, and, when hot, fry the garlic until golden. Do not let it turn brown or the oil may taste bitter.

6 **TOSS** in the meat or shrimp and noodles from the bowl, then stir over high heat briefly, adding sufficient reserved cooking liquid to moisten the noodles and meat or shrimp. The mixture should be moist but not overly wet.

7 **ADD** the bean sprouts, scallions, fish sauce, sugar, and seasoning to taste.

8 **PLACE** in hot serving bowls and sprinkle on the powdered dried shrimp, if using, and an abundance of cilantro leaves for a garnish.

9 **SERVE** with a bowl of sweet chili dipping sauce to drizzle over each helping.

PART 2

THE RECIPES

*Thai cooking is fun, and real **pleasure** is to be had from both cooking and eating Thai dishes. Whether you prepare a **tasty** appetizer, a crisp stir-fry, a slow-cooked curry, or a melt-in-the-mouth dessert, the **flavors** of Thailand will awaken your tastebuds and transport you to the **East**. And you will be amazed at how easy many of these recipes are. With just a few **ingredients** and a quick cooking method, such as stir-frying, you can have a tasty **oriental** meal on the table in no time at all. Classic **favorites** such as Chicken Satay and Thai Fish Cakes intermingle here with less familiar **dishes**, such as Pumpkin and Coconut Cream Soup, Jungle Curry, Steamed Stuffed Crabs, and Mango Sherbet—all of which will **delight** the palate.*

*When **serving** Thai food, it is usual to have a large bowl of fluffy rice in the center of the table. Each diner then takes a **portion** of rice and a little helping from each of the dishes in turn. **Soups** are sipped throughout the meal instead of being served first. Simple **desserts**, which are often fruit based, round off the meal. Such a combination of tastes and textures makes Thai food **unbeatable**.*

SHRIMP TOASTS *KANOM PANG NAH-GOONG*

MAKES 24   PREPARATION TIME: 30 MINUTES
COOKING TIME: 12–15 MINUTES

A stunning blend of pork fat and shrimp with traditional Thai flavorings and a hint of crunchy water chestnut, spread on bread triangles, deep-fried to a golden crunchiness, and served with a sweet and sour cucumber relish.

6 slices **bread**, 2–3 days old

2 teaspoons **sesame seeds**

sunflower oil for deep-frying

1 recipe quantity **Thai relish** (*see page 28*)

TOPPING:

2 ounces **pork fat** (small cubes from the butcher)

½ pound shelled cooked **shrimp**

6 **water chestnuts**

2 **cilantro** stems

1 **garlic** clove, crushed

1 tablespoon **fish sauce**

1 teaspoon **sugar**

1 tablespoon **cornstarch**

1 **egg white**, lightly beaten

salt and freshly ground **black pepper**

1 **BLEND** the cubes of pork fat in a food processor for a few seconds, then add the shrimp and other topping ingredients, and blend to a smooth paste.

2 **SPREAD** the mixture on to the bread slices. Trim the crusts and cut each slice into four triangles or squares. Scatter with the sesame seeds, pressing them in lightly.

3 **PLACE** on a tray lined with baking parchment paper, adding more paper between the toasts to prevent them from sticking to each other. If not being cooked immediately, cover loosely with plastic wrap and refrigerate until required. (If the shrimp were frozen, use the mixture soon after preparation.)

4 **HEAT** the oil in a wok or deep saucepan to 375°F and fry several pieces at a time, paste side down, until crisp and golden, turning once. Drain on paper towels and serve with a little relish spooned on top.

STEAMED DUMPLINGS

KANOM JEEB

MAKES **30**   PREPARATION TIME: **30** MINUTES
COOKING TIME: **20–24** MINUTES

Tiny, light, and luscious dumplings packed with fresh pork, or shrimp, or crunchy vegetables, expertly flavored with cilantro, garlic, soy sauce, and zingy fresh chili, served with a traditional Thai soy dipping sauce.

⅓ pound finely ground **pork**

2 ounces shelled raw **shrimp**, or 4–6 **water chestnuts**, or 1 small **carrot**, finely grated

1 **garlic** clove, crushed

1 **cilantro** stem

1 tablespoon **soy sauce**

1 **red** or **green chili**, seeded and finely chopped

salt and freshly ground **black pepper**

1 **egg**, beaten

30 **wonton wrappers** (3 inches square), thawed if frozen

1 recipe quantity **dark soy dipping sauce** (*see page 27*)

1 PLACE the pork in a food processor with the shrimp, water chestnuts, or carrot, garlic, cilantro stalk and leaves, soy sauce, chili, and seasoning. Blend to a smooth paste with half the beaten egg.

2 PLACE two wrappers at a time on a clean work surface, covering the other wrappers with a damp cloth. Place a tiny spoonful of the mixture on each wrapper.

3 BRUSH lightly around the edge of the wrapper with the remaining beaten egg, then pull up the edges to form a purse shape. Press to seal. If preparing ahead, place the dumplings in a single layer on a tray, cover loosely with plastic wrap, and chill, or freeze, until needed.

4 CUT a sheet of nonstick baking parchment paper into strips and place the dumplings on these in a steamer. Cook the dumplings in two batches over boiling water 10–12 minutes if cooking from fresh (14–16 minutes if cooking from frozen).

5 SERVE hot with the soy dipping sauce.

THAI EGG ROLLS *POW-PIA TAWD*

**MAKES 12   PREPARATION TIME: 25 MINUTES, PLUS 20–30 MINUTES
SOAKING TIME   COOKING TIME: 8–10 MINUTES**

*Dainty, crisp, golden rolls encasing a sumptuous mixture of Chinese mushrooms,
bean sprouts, tender chicken or pork, and noodles, served with a sharp plum sauce.*

24 **egg roll wrappers** (5 inches square), thawed if frozen

½ **egg**, beaten

cornstarch (optional)

sunflower oil for deep-frying

1 recipe quantity **preserved plum dipping sauce** (*see page 27*)

FILLING:

4 **Chinese mushrooms**

1 ounce **bean thread noodles**

3 tablespoons **sunflower oil**

6 ounces finely ground **chicken** breast or **pork**

1 cup **bean sprouts**

1 **carrot**, finely grated

1 **garlic** clove, crushed

2 **cilantro** stems, stalks and leaves chopped

salt and freshly ground **black pepper**

1 **SOAK** the mushrooms in warm water 20–30 minutes, then drain, discard the stems, and slice the mushroom caps very finely. Meanwhile, soak the noodles in warm water 10 minutes until soft, then drain, and cut into small pieces with scissors.

2 **HEAT** a wok, add the 3 tablespoons of oil, then the chicken or pork, and stir-fry 2–3 minutes. Add the remaining filling ingredients and toss well over moderate heat 2–3 minutes. Put on a plate and let cool.

3 **PLACE** two egg roll wrappers at a time on a clean work surface, covering the others with a damp cloth. Place a spoonful of filling on each wrapper and roll up one turn.

4 **TURN** the sides to the middle and continue rolling into a neat shape, brushing a little beaten egg on to the tip to seal each egg roll.

5 **PLACE** in a single layer on a clean plate dusted lightly with a little cornstarch or on a sheet of nonstick baking parchment paper.

6 **HEAT** the oil for deep-frying to 375°F. Deep-fry several egg rolls at a time until golden. This will take 2 minutes. Drain on plenty of paper towels. Serve hot with the preserved plum dipping sauce.

SHRIMP SATAY *GOONG SATAY*

MAKES **16**   PREPARATION TIME: **10** MINUTES, PLUS **30** MINUTES
MARINATING TIME   COOKING TIME: **3–4** MINUTES

---

2 teaspoons **sugar**

6 **cilantro** stems, stalks only

1 **garlic** clove

½-inch piece fresh **ginger**, peeled and sliced

½ **green chili**, seeded and finely shredded

3 tablespoons **sunflower oil**

16 large raw **shrimp**, heads removed, shelled,
  but tails left on

1 recipe quantity **peanut sauce** (*see page 28*)
  to serve

lettuce leaves and chunks of **cucumber**
  to serve

1 SOAK 16 bamboo or wooden skewers in water to cover.

2 PLACE the sugar, cilantro stalks, garlic, ginger, and chili in a mortar with the oil and use a pestle to pound to a fragrant paste. Pour the paste over the shrimp, mix thoroughly, and let marinate 30 minutes while you make the peanut sauce.

3 THREAD the shrimp on to the soaked skewers. Place under a hot broiler until the shrimp are pink and cooked, turning as necessary. Allow about 3–4 minutes only.

4 SERVE with the peanut sauce and chunks of cucumber on a lettuce-lined serving dish.

VARIATION **CHICKEN, PORK, AND BEEF SATAY** *GAI, MOO* AND *NEAU SATAY*

Chill ½ pound each of chicken breast, lean pork, and filet mignon in the freezer 30 minutes before cutting into neat, even-size pieces, keeping the meats separate. Prepare the marinade by stirring 1 cup coconut milk, 1 teaspoon ground turmeric, 1 teaspoon hot or mild curry powder to taste, and a pinch of salt together. Pour this over the chicken and pork pieces. For the beef satay, sprinkle the meat with ground cumin before pouring the marinade over it. Let all the meats marinate at least 1 hour. Thread the meats separately on to soaked wooden skewers just before cooking. Cook under a hot broiler or over a barbecue, brushing with some of the marinade. Turn frequently until cooked through. Serve on a large plate with peanut sauce (*see page 28*) and cucumber salad (*see page 146*) or pieces of onion and cucumber.

THAI FISH CAKES *TAWD MUN PLA*

**MAKES 24   PREPARATION TIME: 20–25 MINUTES
COOKING TIME: 10–12 MINUTES**

Delicate little fish cakes, crisp and golden on the outside, moist and tasty on the inside, flavored with red curry paste, string beans, lime leaves, and fish sauce.

1¼ pound **cod** or **haddock** fillet

2 teaspoons **red curry paste** (*see page 24*)

1 tablespoon **fish sauce**

2 tablespoons **cornstarch**

2 ounces **long** or **string beans**, finely sliced

3 **lime leaves**, very finely shredded

½ **egg**, beaten

salt and freshly ground **black pepper**

sunflower oil, to cover base of pan

8 **lemongrass** stems, top parts only

CRUNCHY SWEET CHILI SAUCE:

4 tablespoons **sweet chili dipping sauce**
  (*see page 27*)

½ small **carrot**, finely diced

1-inch piece **cucumber**, finely diced

2 **cilantro** stems, leaves roughly torn

2 tablespoons roasted **peanuts**, lightly crushed

1 **SKIN** and bone the fish, then cut into pieces and process briefly in a food processor. Add the curry paste, fish sauce, cornstarch, beans, and lime leaves, then process again briefly. Finally, add just sufficient beaten egg to bind the mixture. Season well.

2 **FORM** into even-size fish cakes with a hole in the center. Chill, if time allows, or freeze for future use if required.

3 **PUT** the dipping sauce in a serving bowl. Add the carrot and cucumber and add a few torn cilantro leaves. Cover and chill. Stir in the lightly crushed peanuts and remaining cilantro leaves just before serving.

4 **SHALLOW-FRY** the fish cakes in hot oil 2–3 minutes on each side (3–4 minutes if frozen), depending on the size.

5 **THREAD** three fish cakes on to each lemongrass stem and serve with the sauce, to be spooned on to each fish cake in turn.

SHRIMP IN BLANKETS *KUNG HOM PA*

MAKES 16 **PREPARATION TIME: 25 MINUTES**
COOKING TIME: 6–10 MINUTES

This is a variation on the egg roll. You need large fresh shrimp with tails intact so that they project out of one end of the roll. The shrimp are cut in half to hasten the cooking then combined with a spicy, crunchy pork stuffing.

16 raw **jumbo shrimp**, heads removed, shelled, but tails left on

16 **egg roll wrappers** (5 inches square), thawed if frozen

½ **egg**, beaten

sunflower oil for deep-frying

1 recipe quantity **sweet chili dipping sauce** (*see page 27*)

STUFFING:

2 ounces ground **pork**

6 **water chestnuts**

1 **scallion**, chopped

½-inch piece fresh **ginger**, peeled and sliced

1 teaspoon **fish sauce**

freshly ground **black pepper**

1 **CUT** each shrimp in half along the back, then open out, removing the vein if necessary.

2 **PREPARE** the stuffing. Mix the pork, water chestnuts, scallion, ginger, and fish sauce in a food processor with pepper to make a fine paste.

3 **SPREAD** out four egg roll wrappers on a clean work surface, covering the others with a damp cloth, and place a small spoonful of stuffing on each wrapper near the lower edge. Lay a shrimp on top of the stuffing with the tail exposed.

4 **FOLD** each wrapper over toward the tail, then brush the edges with beaten egg, and roll up, with the shrimp tail exposed. Make up the remainder of the rolls in the same way and place in a single layer on a tray lined with baking parchment paper.

5 **HEAT** the oil for deep-frying in a wok or deep saucepan to 375°F, and fry several of the wrapped shrimp at a time 2–3 minutes until golden. Drain on crumpled paper towels.

6 **SERVE** with a bowl of sweet chili dipping sauce alongside.

NAM PRIK SAUCE WITH CRUDITES

NAM PRIK PAK JEEM

SERVES **4–5**   PREPARATION TIME: **15** MINUTES, PLUS **15** MINUTES SOAKING TIME

In Thailand this is the universal sauce. It is used as a dip and is usually served with a colorful selection of fresh vegetable "dippers" and some puffy shrimp chips. The sauce can also be served simply stirred into a bowl of rice as a light meal.

2 ounces **dried shrimp**

½-inch cube prepared **kapi** *(see page 15)*

2–3 **garlic** cloves, crushed

1–3 **red** or **green chilies**, seeded and chopped

2 ounces shelled cooked **shrimp**

1 large **cilantro** stem

12 tiny **pea eggplants**

2 tablespoons **fish sauce**

3–4 tablespoons **lemon juice**

1 tablespoon **dark brown sugar**

selection of **vegetable crudités**, such as cucumber, carrot, celery, tomato, plus shrimp chips and pork crackling *(see page 18)*

1 **SOAK** the dried shrimp in water 15 minutes, then drain. Place them with the prepared kapi, garlic, and chilies (the number depending on how hot you like your food) in a food processor and blend.

2 **ADD** the shrimp and most of the cilantro stalks and leaves, reserving some of the leaves for a garnish. Add the eggplants and process again. Now add the seasonings of fish sauce, lemon juice, and sugar to taste. Add a little water if you feel that the sauce is too thick, but this should not be necessary.

3 **ARRANGE** the selected vegetables, the shrimp chips, and pork crackling attractively on a serving dish and place the sauce in a bowl in the center for dipping. This can be made up in advance, covered in plastic wrap, and chilled until required.

4 **GARNISH** the sauce with the reserved cilantro leaves just before serving. (Any leftover sauce can be stored in a glass screwtop jar with plastic wrap under the lid for a week.)

SHRIMP CHIPS

KHOW GRIEB GOONG

SERVES 4   PREPARATION TIME: 2 MINUTES   COOKING TIME: 4–5 MINUTES

*Crisp, light-as-air chips, ready to dip into sweet chili dipping sauce (*nam prik waan*), tangy yet sweet preserved plum dipping sauce (*nam bouy*), and dark soy dipping sauce (*si-ew waan*), make a delicious predinner nibble with drinks.*

---

sunflower oil for deep-frying

2–3 ounces uncooked **shrimp chips**

selection of **dipping sauces** *(see page 27)*

1 **HEAT** the oil in a wok or deep saucepan to 375ºF. Line a tray with a double layer of crumpled paper towels.

2 **DEEP-FRY** only 8–10 shrimp chips at a time, since they swell up considerably in size. Keep them moving as they cook, which will take only 10–20 seconds. Take care not to cook in oil that is too hot. They should remain white or pale pink after cooking.

3 **LIFT** out with a slotted spoon and drain on paper towels. Serve with any or all of the dipping sauces on page 27. Any leftovers keep well in an airtight plastic container.

MONEY BAGS *THUNG THONG*

MAKES 20   PREPARATION TIME: 30 MINUTES, PLUS 20–30 MINUTES SOAKING TIME   COOKING TIME: 9–12 MINUTES

---

40 **egg roll wrappers** (5 inches square), thawed if frozen

½ **egg**, beaten

sunflower oil for deep-frying

1 recipe quantity **sweet chili dipping sauce** (*see page 27*)

FILLING:

3 **Chinese mushrooms**

1 ounce **bean thread noodles**

1 **garlic** clove

8 **black peppercorns**

2 **cilantro** stems

½ pound ground **pork**

¼ pound shelled cooked **shrimp**

1 teaspoon **sugar**

1 tablespoon **fish sauce**

5 **scallions** with long green tops, green parts only

1 SOAK the Chinese mushrooms in warm water 20–30 minutes, then drain. Remove the stems and slice the caps finely. Meanwhile, soak the bean thread noodles in warm water 10 minutes until soft, then drain.

2 POUND the garlic, peppercorns, and cilantro stalks and roots (if available) together, reserving the cilantro leaves for a garnish.

3 MIX the ground pork with the shrimp in a food processor. Place in a bowl. With scissors, snip the bean thread noodles into short lengths.

4 HEAT the oil and fry the cilantro mixture until it gives off a fragrant aroma. Add the pork, shrimp, noodles, and mushrooms. Cook 3–4 minutes until the pork is cooked, stirring and tossing so that the mixture is well broken up. Add the sugar and fish sauce. Remove from the heat and let cool.

5 PLUNGE the long green tops of the scallions into boiling water, then put directly into cold water. Drain well and set aside.

6 USE two wrappers for each money bag. Place one square in front of you and one with the points over the straight sides. Place a small spoonful of filling in the center of each stack, brush the edge with beaten egg to seal, then form into a sack shape. Tie attractively with the drained scallion tops and secure with a cocktail stick if necessary.

7 HEAT the oil for deep-frying in a work or deep saucepan to 375ºF, then deep-fry the money bags in batches 3 minutes, or until crispy and golden brown. Lift out and drain on paper towels.

8 PLACE on a serving dish and serve with the sweet chili dipping sauce.

CORN CAKES

TAWD MUN KOW POD

**MAKES 24   PREPARATION TIME: 30 MINUTES
COOKING TIME: 6–8 MINUTES**

Tender ground pork, juicy corn, fragrant lime leaves, and a dash of red curry paste, blended together to make mouth-watering, crisp-fried morsels topped with the wonderful contrasting flavors of a sweet spicy dipping sauce or Thai relish.

1½ cups canned **corn**, drained

⅔ pound finely ground **pork**

2 teaspoons **red curry paste** (*see page 24*)

1 tablespoon **soy sauce**

3 tablespoons **cornstarch**

4 **lime leaves**, finely shredded

1 **cilantro** stem

2 teaspoons **sugar**

½ **egg**, beaten

sunflower oil

lettuce leaves to serve

1 recipe quantity **sweet chili dipping sauce** or **Thai relish** (*see pages 27 or 28*)

1 **PLACE** the corn in a bowl with the pork, curry paste, soy sauce, cornstarch, and shredded lime leaves. Chop the cilantro stalk (reserving the leaves for a garnish) and add to the mixture.

2 **BLEND** together well by hand, then add the sugar, and slowly add just sufficient beaten egg to bind.

3 **FORM** into small cakes, using the flat blade of a knife lightly brushed with oil, and place on a well-floured tray.

4 **SHALLOW-FRY** about 3–5 minutes in hot oil on both sides until brown and cooked through. Drain on paper towels.

5 **GARNISH** with the cilantro leaves and serve with lettuce. Spoon a little sauce or relish on to each corn cake before eating.

LETTUCE PACKAGES

MIENG KAM OR *KHANA HAW*

SERVES 4   PREPARATION TIME: 25 MINUTES

A dish of fresh lettuce leaves, wafer-thin lemon, shredded chili and ginger, crunchy salted peanuts, and plump shrimp. Allow your guests to make up their own packages using as much or as little of the spices as their taste buds will allow.

8 **lettuce leaves** from a round, soft lettuce

4 paper-thin slices of **lemon**, quartered

1 **red** and 1 **green chili**, shredded

1-inch piece fresh **ginger**, shredded

1 handful salted **peanuts**

32 shelled cooked **shrimp** or 16 shelled cooked **tiger shrimp** (can be cut in half)

8 small **lemon** wedges

1 **PLACE** the lettuce leaves, which must be completely dry, in one bowl and divide the remaining ingredients into four small piles or ramekins on a central serving dish.

2 **INVITE** each diner to place a lettuce leaf on their plate, place half the filling ingredients on top, and finish with a squeeze of lemon. The leaf should then be rolled up into a neat package and eaten at once, before the second lettuce package is made with the remaining ingredients.

COCONUT CRISPS *MAPRAOW KRUA*

MAKES 1 POUND   PREPARATION TIME: 25 MINUTES
COOKING TIME: 30 MINUTES

This recipe for coconut crisps may sound as if a lot of effort is required,
but the enthusiasm of your guests will make it all worthwhile.

1 large fresh **coconut**

2 tablespoons **sea salt**

1 **HEAT** the oven to 325°F.

2 **OPEN** the coconut (see page 12) and use a knife to ease the two halves apart. Crack into smaller pieces if necessary.

3 **SLIDE** the blade of a palette knife between the white flesh and brown husk of the coconut to ease away the hard outer casing. If you prefer to remove the remaining brown skin, do so using a vegetable peeler, but this is not essential.

4 **FIT** the fine-slicing blade attachment to your food processor, then feed the peeled pieces of coconut down the feed tube. (If not all the coconut slices are required now, place the remainder on an open tray and freeze for future use.)

5 **PLACE** the thin coconut slices on a baking sheet, sprinkle with salt, and bake in the heated oven 30 minutes. Turn twice to insure even cooking. Cool before serving.

BEEF SOUP WITH NOODLES

GUAY TIEW NAM-NEAU

SERVES 4   PREPARATION TIME: 20 MINUTES   COOKING TIME: 35 MINUTES

Rice noodles, tender beef strips, and crunchy bean sprouts gently submerged in a rich, garlicky beef stock with the warm fragrances of cinnamon and kha.

4 cups **beef stock** or diluted **consommé**

3 **cilantro** stems

½ bunch **scallions**, finely chopped

½-inch piece **kha**, bruised

1 **cinnamon** stick

¼ pound **flat dried rice noodles**
   or ½ pound **flat fresh rice noodles**

2 tablespoons **sunflower oil**

¼ pound **filet mignon**, lightly frozen,
   then cut into matchsticks

1 **garlic** clove, crushed

1–2 tablespoons **fish sauce**

1 tablespoon **dark soy sauce**

juice of ½ **lemon** or **lime**

freshly ground **black pepper**

¼ cup **bean sprouts**

1 small **red** or **green chili**, finely sliced

1 **POUR** the stock into a saucepan. Crush the cilantro stalks (reserving the leaves for a garnish) and add along with half the scallions, the kha, and cinnamon stick. Bring to a boil, then turn the heat down and simmer 20 minutes. Remove the kha and cinnamon stick.

2 **SOAK** the flat dried rice noodles, if using, in warm water 15 minutes while the stock is simmering, then drain.

3 **HEAT** the oil in a skillet and fry the beef strips and garlic until the beef changes color. Add to the stock along with the fish sauce to taste, the soy sauce, lemon or lime juice, and pepper to taste. Bring to a boil and simmer 5 minutes. Taste again and adjust the seasoning if necessary.

4 **PLACE** the drained dried rice noodles, if using, in a large saucepan of boiling water and cook 2 minutes. Drain well, rinse through with boiling water in a colander. If using fresh rice noodles, cut into fine strips and plunge into boiling water 1 minute. Drain, rinse, and drain again.

5 **DIVIDE** the noodles and bean sprouts between four soup bowls. Spoon over the hot soup and garnish with the remaining scallions, cilantro leaves, and shredded chilies.

CLEAR SOUP WITH STUFFED MUSHROOMS

GAENG JUED HED

SERVES 4   PREPARATION TIME: 12–15 MINUTES, PLUS 20–30 MINUTES SOAKING TIME   COOKING TIME: 15 MINUTES

Chinese mushrooms stuffed with a mixture of pork, garlic, cilantro, scallions, and crunchy water chestnuts, moistened with soy sauce then steamed and served in a full-bodied chicken stock laced with fish sauce.

8 small **Chinese mushrooms,** or **Shiitake,** or **button mushrooms**

4 cups **chicken stock** (*see page 23*)

1–2 tablespoons **fish sauce**

1 handful young **spinach** leaves

STUFFING:

2 ounces finely ground **pork** with some pork fat

½ **garlic** clove, crushed

1 **cilantro** stem

½–1 teaspoon **soy sauce**

1 **scallion**, chopped

3 **water chestnuts**

salt and freshly ground **black pepper**

1 **SOAK** the mushrooms in ⅔ cup warm water 20–30 minutes. Pour the soaking water into a saucepan with the stock. (If using fresh mushrooms, add extra vegetable stock or water.)

2 **DISCARD** the stems from the Chinese mushrooms and leave the caps whole. Remove the stems from the button mushrooms, if using.

3 **PLACE** the pork in a food processor with the garlic and cilantro stalks (reserve the leaves for a garnish). Add the soy sauce, scallion, water chestnuts, and seasoning, then process to a paste.

4 **DIVIDE** the mixture between the mushrooms. Place on strips of nonstick baking parchment paper in a bamboo or metal steamer over boiling water, cover, and steam 15 minutes.

5 **BRING** the stock to a boil in the meantime. Add the fish sauce and season to taste.

6 **PLACE** the steamed mushrooms in soup bowls with the cilantro leaves and tiny pieces of torn spinach and pour over the boiling stock.

CLEAR SOUP WITH WONTONS *GIEW NAM*

SERVES 6   PREPARATION TIME: 25–35 MINUTES
COOKING TIME: 6 MINUTES

A steaming bowl of tiny dumplings filled with a sumptuous mixture of pork or shrimp, garlic, cilantro, and fish sauce, topped with crunchy bean sprouts or finely shredded Chinese leaves, floating in a rich fish or chicken stock.

¼ pound lean ground **pork** or shelled cooked **shrimp**

½ **garlic** clove, crushed

2 **cilantro** stems

2 teaspoons **soy** or **fish sauce**

freshly ground **black pepper**

½ **egg**, beaten

18 **wonton wrappers** (3 inches square), thawed if frozen

6 cups **chicken** or **fish stock** (*see page 23*)

generous 1 cup **bean sprouts** or finely shredded **Chinese leaves**

1 **green chili**, seeded and finely chopped to garnish

1 **BLEND** the pork or shrimp with the garlic and cilantro stalks (reserving the leaves for garnish) in a food processor. When smooth, add the soy or fish sauce, pepper, and just enough egg to bind, reserving the remainder for sealing the wontons.

2 **PLACE** several wonton wrappers at a time on a clean work surface (covering the rest with a damp cloth) and place a tiny spoonful of the mixture on each one. Brush the edges with a little of the beaten egg.

3 **FOLD** into purse shapes, sealing the tops well. Alternatively, roll up into mini egg-roll shapes, damping the last edges to seal. Whichever shape you choose, the wontons should be bite size.

4 **LEAVE** covered until required. If they are to be kept for a while, place them on baking parchment paper so that they will not stick to the surface of the plate or box.

5 **BRING** a saucepan of water to a boil and cook the wontons in this in two batches 3 minutes. Meanwhile, bring the stock to a boil.

6 **LIFT** the wontons out of the water with a slotted spoon and divide between six soup bowls. Top with the bean sprouts or shredded Chinese leaves and pour over the boiling soup. Serve garnished with chopped chili and the reserved cilantro leaves.

CHICKEN SOUP WITH COCONUT

TOM KHA GAI

**SERVES 4   PREPARATION TIME: 8–10 MINUTES
COOKING TIME: 12–15 MINUTES**

This fragrant, creamy textured soup, with its thin slivers of tender chicken, has a deceptive bite from the fresh red chilies nestling in its midst. Stop to smell the fabulous blend of aromas before you take the first spoonful.

1⅔ cups canned **coconut milk**

generous 2 cups **chicken stock** (*see page 23*)

1¼ cups **water**

¾-inch piece **kha**, peeled and finely sliced

2 **red chilies**, seeded and sliced

1 **lemongrass** stem, lower 2½ inches sliced

3 **lime leaves**, torn in pieces

4 tablespoons **fish sauce**

2 tablespoons **lemon** juice

1 teaspoon **sugar**

1 **chicken** breast (about 6 ounces), cut into slivers

cilantro leaves to garnish

1 **POUR** the coconut milk into a saucepan, stirring over gentle heat to make sure that the milk is smooth. Stir in one direction only to prevent the milk curdling.

2 **HEAT** the prepared stock in a much larger saucepan with the water, kha, chilies, lemongrass, and torn lime leaves.

3 **STIR** in the warmed coconut milk, then add the fish sauce, lemon juice, and sugar. Allow to come to a boil, then reduce the heat and simmer 5 minutes. Taste and adjust the seasoning.

4 **BRING** back to a boil, drop in the chicken slivers a few at a time so that they remain separate. Cook 3–4 minutes until the chicken pieces are cooked.

5 **SERVE** garnished with cilantro leaves.

CHIANG MAI CURRIED NOODLE SOUP WITH CHICKEN *KHAO SOI GAI*

SERVES 4   PREPARATION TIME: 35 MINUTES   COOKING TIME: 30 MINUTES

1 **chicken** (2¾ pounds), skinned

2½ cups canned **coconut milk**

1–2 tablespoons **red curry paste** (*see page 24*)

1 teaspoon **ground turmeric**

generous 3 cups **chicken stock** (*see page 23*)

2–3 tablespoons **fish sauce**

2 tablespoons **soy sauce**

juice of 1 **lime**

1 handful **cilantro leaves**, roughly chopped

1 pound **fresh** or **dried egg noodles** (if using dried, soak for 10 minutes)

GARNISHES:

2 ounces **dried egg noodles**

1–2 **red chilies**, seeded and finely sliced

4 **shallots**, finely sliced

4 **scallions**, sliced at an angle

1 can **fermented mustard greens** (5 ounces), finely sliced

1 **CUT** the chicken meat into bite-size pieces. (The legs can be kept in the refrigerator for use in another recipe.)

2 **POUR** 1½ cups coconut milk into a wok or large saucepan. Stir over medium heat until the milk begins to curdle, then add the curry paste and turmeric. Stir to make a rich sauce, then reduce the heat, and cook 3 minutes.

3 **ADD** the chicken and turn it in the spicy mixture until well coated. Pour in the remaining coconut milk, stock, fish sauce to taste, and soy sauce, then cook over medium heat 8 minutes until the chicken is tender. Add the lime juice and scatter with the cilantro leaves.

4 **PREPARE** the garnishes by deep-frying the noodles until crisp. Drain on paper towels, then lightly crush to add texture and crunch to the soup. Place with the other garnishes in small ramekins.

5 **PLUNGE** the fresh noodles into boiling water, then drain. If using dried noodles, place them in boiling salted water. Return to a boil and cook 5 minutes or according to the package directions. Drain, rinse with boiling water, and drain again.

6 **PLACE** the noodles in warm bowls and pour on the soup. Top with cilantro leaves and some crushed fried noodles.

7 **HAND** around the other garnishes at the table.

HOT AND SOUR SHRIMP SOUP *TOM YUM GOONG*

SERVES 4   PREPARATION TIME: 15 MINUTES
COOKING TIME: 18–20 MINUTES

Shrimp and squid are gently simmered in homemade stock, flavored with the delicate fragrance of lemongrass, kha, lime leaves, and the essential fish sauce, before being garnished with thinly sliced red chili and fresh cilantro.

3 cups **fish** or **chicken stock** (*see page 23*)

1¼ cups **water**

1 **lemongrass** stem

4 **red bird's eye chilies**, seeded and finely sliced

1-inch piece **kha**, peeled and finely sliced

3 **lime leaves**, torn into pieces

2–3 ready-cleaned **squid**

12 shelled cooked **tiger shrimp** or ½ pound small shelled cooked **shrimp**

1 can **straw mushrooms** (½ pound), drained or 4 **button mushrooms**, sliced

juice of 1 large **lemon**

1 teaspoon **sugar**

2–3 tablespoons **fish sauce**

1 **red chili**, seeded and finely sliced to garnish

cilantro leaves to garnish

1 PLACE the stock in a large saucepan with the water. Heat gently.

2 TRIM the root from the lemongrass and slice the bottom 2-inch section into fine slices. Bruise the remaining stalk and add all this to the stock with the chilies, kha, and two of the torn lime leaves.

3 BRING to a boil, reduce the heat, and simmer gently 10 minutes to blend all the flavors.

4 PREPARE the squid and cut into strips or rings (see page 19).

5 REMOVE the bruised lemongrass, add the shrimp, squid, and the mushrooms, then add the lemon juice, sugar, and fish sauce a little at a time, testing as you do, until you have the right balance of flavors.

6 SERVE in bowls with slices of red chili, the remaining torn lime leaf, and a few cilantro leaves floating on top.

MIXED SEAFOOD AND COCONUT SOUP

TOM KHA TALAY

SERVES 4   PREPARATION TIME: 20 MINUTES   COOKING TIME: 10 MINUTES

Cod, squid, and shrimp cooked in a spiced stock blended with coconut milk and flavored with turmeric—a seafood soup to remember.

⅓ pound **cod**, skinned and cut into cubes

⅓ pound ready-cleaned **squid**

12 shelled cooked **tiger shrimp**

1⅔ cups canned **coconut milk**

1 teaspoon **ground turmeric**

3 cups **fish stock** (*see page 23*)

1¼ cups **water**

2 **lemongrass** stems, lower 2½ inches finely sliced

¾-inch piece **kha**, peeled and finely sliced

3 **lime leaves**, torn

2 **red** or **green chilies**, seeded and finely sliced

4 tablespoons **fish sauce**

3 tablespoons **lime** or **lemon** juice

1–2 **dried chilies**, seeded and broken into pieces

1 small handful **cilantro leaves**

1 **ASSEMBLE** the fresh fish pieces and seafood, which should total just over a pound. Prepare the squid and cut into rings or strips (see page 19). Arrange on a plate, cover, and chill.

2 **POUR** one-third of the coconut milk into a saucepan. Heat gently and, when bubbling, add the turmeric and cook 1 minute, stirring all the time, to bring out the flavor. Stir in the remaining coconut milk and mix thoroughly until all the coconut is incorporated and smooth. Remove from the heat.

3 **HEAT** the stock and water in a separate saucepan. Add the lemongrass, kha, lime leaves, and chilies. Bring to a boil and simmer 5 minutes to bring out the flavor.

4 **ADD** the coconut milk and turmeric mixture, the fish sauce, and lime or lemon juice. Taste for seasoning.

5 **BRING** the soup to a boil, add the fish pieces and seafood, return to a boil, then turn the heat down and simmer 3–4 minutes only.

6 **SERVE** at once, garnished with the dried chilies and cilantro leaves.

PUMPKIN AND COCONUT CREAM SOUP

GAENG LIANG FAK TONG

SERVES **4**   PREPARATION TIME: **12** MINUTES, PLUS **15** MINUTES
SOAKING TIME   COOKING TIME: **30** MINUTES

An unusual soup that gets its creamy texture from blending spices and dried shrimp into a liquid paste. If you wish, add some fresh shrimp just before serving.

2 ounces **dried shrimp**

⅔ cup warm **water**

1 **onion**, quartered

¾-inch piece fresh **ginger**, peeled

2 **red** or **green chilies**, seeded

1 **lemongrass** stem, lower 2½ inches cut in three and top of stem bruised

1⅓ cups **chicken** or **fish stock** (*see page 23*) or **water**

1⅔ cups canned **coconut milk**

2 tablespoons **fish sauce**

1 teaspoon **sugar**

freshly ground **black pepper**

1 pound **pumpkin**, peeled, seeded, and diced

1 small handful **basil leaves**

¼ pound shelled cooked **shrimp** (optional)

1 SOAK the dried shrimp in the warm water 15 minutes.

2 PROCESS the onion, ginger, chilies, and the lower part of the lemongrass with the soaked shrimp and their liquid in a food processor until well blended.

3 POUR the stock or water into a large saucepan and add the coconut milk. Combine well.

4 HEAT until nearly boiling, then pour in the spice mixture, and stir over gentle heat until the soup is well blended. Add the fish sauce to taste, the sugar, and black pepper.

5 RETURN to a boil, then turn the heat down, and simmer the soup 5 minutes. Add the pumpkin dice, lemongrass stem, and some basil leaves (reserve a few to garnish). Cook a further 20 minutes, stirring from time to time and checking with a skewer to see whether the pumpkin is tender. Remove the lemongrass stem. Add the shelled shrimp, if using.

6 SERVE hot in bowls with the remaining basil leaves, torn.

HOT AND SOUR VEGETABLE SOUP

TOM YUM PAK

SERVES 4   PREPARATION TIME: 5—8 MINUTES   COOKING TIME: 15 MINUTES

A stunningly colorful clear soup full of stir-fried baby corn, mushrooms, carrots, and spinach, laced with lemon or lime, lemongrass, and kha and spiked with chilies.

---

4 cups **vegetable** or **chicken stock**
(*see page 23*)

1¼ cups **water**

2 **lemongrass** stems, lower 2 inches sliced

½-inch piece **kha**, scraped and finely sliced

2 **chilies**, seeded and sliced

2 **cilantro** stems

3 **lime leaves**, torn in pieces

1–2 tablespoons **fish sauce**

juice of 1–2 **limes** or 1 large **lemon**

salt and freshly ground **black pepper**

1 teaspoon **sugar**

4 **baby corn**, finely sliced

8 **button mushrooms**, finely sliced

1 **carrot**, finely diced

2 tablespoons **sunflower oil**

1 handful **spinach**, shredded

1 **POUR** the stock and water into a large saucepan, add the lemongrass, kha, and one of the chilies, chopped cilantro stalks (reserve the leaves for garnish), and the lime leaves.

2 **BRING** to a boil, then reduce the heat to simmer 10 minutes. Add the fish sauce and sufficient lime or lemon juice to give a tart flavor. Taste as you add the lime or lemon juice to get the right balance of flavor. Adjust the seasoning and add a little sugar if liked.

3 **ASSEMBLE** the prepared vegetables (apart from the spinach) in a large bowl. Heat the oil in a saucepan, add the vegetables, and toss everything together 1 minute.

4 **ADD** to the boiling soup, adding the spinach at the last moment in order to retain its rich color.

5 **GARNISH** the soup with the reserved cilantro leaves and the remaining chili, if liked.

THAI BEEF SALAD *YUM NEAU*

**SERVES 4   PREPARATION TIME: 15–20 MINUTES
COOKING TIME: 4–6 MINUTES**

Filet mignon, perfectly cooked to a delicate pink, then cut into wafer-thin slices, tossed with matchsticks of carrot and cucumber, thinly sliced red onion, scallions, and a tangy yet fiery dressing, garnished with mint and cilantro.

½ pound **filet mignon**

salt and freshly ground **black pepper**

3 tablespoons **fish sauce**

juice of 1 large **lime** or **lemon**

1 tablespoon **sugar**

1 **red chili**, seeded and finely sliced

4 **shallots** or 1 small **red onion**, finely sliced

2 **garlic** cloves, crushed

2 **lemongrass** stems, lower 2 inches finely sliced

⅓ **cucumber**, cut into matchsticks or coarsely grated

2 **carrots**, cut into matchsticks or coarsely grated

2–3 **scallions**, finely shredded

1 small handful each **cilantro** and **mint leaves**

1 **SEASON** the beef, then place it under a hot broiler. Cook to medium-rare (about 4–6 minutes, depending on thickness), turning twice during cooking. Let rest 10 minutes before slicing thinly.

2 **BLEND** the fish sauce with the lime or lemon juice, sugar, chili, and half the shallots or onion to make the dressing.

3 **TOSS** the beef slices with the garlic, lemongrass slices, remaining shallots or onion, cucumber, carrots, some of the scallions and some of the cilantro, and torn mint leaves. Add the dressing.

4 **PILE** on to a deep serving dish and garnish with the remaining scallion, cilantro, and mint leaves. (If this salad is to be eaten as part of a picnic, dress with just one-third of the dressing and take the remainder with you to pour over at the last minute.)

THANYING SALAD *YUM THANYING*

SERVES 4   PREPARATION TIME: 30 MINUTES   COOKING TIME: 4 MINUTES

Reputed to be a dish revered by the Thai royal family, this mixture of chicken and vegetables folded into a sour, sweet, and salty cucumber relish is certainly fit for a king! This is a specialty from a famous restaurant in Bangkok, The Thanying.

¼ **cucumber**, halved, seeded, then coarsely grated or diced

4 **shallots** or 1 small **red onion**, sliced

2–3 **red chilies**, seeded and sliced

2 tablespoons **light** or **dark brown sugar**

4 tablespoons **rice vinegar**

freshly ground **black pepper**

½ pound **long** or **string beans**, trimmed

2 teaspoons **sesame seeds** to garnish

⅓ cup salted **peanuts**, finely crushed

¾ pound cold cooked **chicken**, cut into fine strips

3 **carrots**, cut into matchsticks

1 cup **bean sprouts**, brown tails removed if necessary

lettuce leaves to garnish

6 **cilantro stems**, leaves chopped to garnish

1 **PLACE** the grated or diced cucumber in a bowl. Pound the shallots or onion and chili to a paste using a mortar and pestle, then add the sugar, vinegar, and pepper. It should taste sour, sweet, and salty.

2 **PLUNGE** the beans into a saucepan of boiling water 2 minutes, then drain, and cut into pieces.

3 **WARM** a skillet, then dry-fry the sesame seeds 2 minutes until golden, moving them all the time to avoid burning.

4 **TOSS** the cucumber and the pounded ingredients together with the peanuts, then fold in the chicken strips, beans, carrots, and bean sprouts just before serving.

5 **PLACE** on a serving dish with some lettuce leaves and garnish with cilantro leaves and the toasted sesame seeds.

SQUID SALAD *YUM PLA MEUK*

**SERVES 4   PREPARATION TIME: 20–25 MINUTES
COOKING TIME: 3 MINUTES**

Rings or attractive curls of squid, stir-fried then marinated in herbs, chilies, fresh lemon, fish sauce, and a good helping of onion and garlic, served on a bed of lettuce. You will find this dish on most restaurant menus.

1 pound ready-cleaned **squid**

juice of 1 large **lemon**

2 tablespoons **fish sauce**

1 **garlic** clove, crushed

1 **red chili**, seeded and finely shredded

1 **lemongrass** stem, lower 2½ inches finely sliced

4 **scallions**, white parts only, shredded

2 **shallots**, finely sliced

2–3 **mint** sprigs, leaves chopped

2 **cilantro** stems, leaves chopped

lettuce leaves to garnish

4 **lime leaves**, finely shredded to garnish

1 **lemon**, cut into 4 wedges to serve

1 **PREPARE** the squid and cut into strips or rings (see page 19); keep the tentacles to one side.

2 **HEAT** a wok, without any oil, toss in the squid rings or strips, and stir-fry 2–3 minutes until the pieces of squid look cooked and are curling. Lift out of the wok with a slotted spoon into a bowl. Repeat with the tentacles.

3 **SPOON** the lemon juice, fish sauce, garlic, chili, and half the lemongrass slices over the squid. Cover with plastic wrap and chill until ready to serve.

4 **ADD** most of the scallions to the fish salad with the shallots just before serving, with some of the mint and cilantro leaves.

5 **LINE** a serving dish with lettuce leaves, place the well-mixed fish on top of this, and garnish with the remaining lemongrass slices, mint and cilantro leaves, and the shredded lime leaves. Provide lemon wedges to squeeze over the dish.

BABY CORN AND SUGAR SNAPS WITH GINGER AND GARLIC *PAD YOD KAO POD KAB KHING*

SERVES 4   PREPARATION TIME: 6–8 MINUTES   COOKING TIME: 5 MINUTES

Vibrantly colored vegetables with zingy ginger and garlic flavors that can be cooked and served in double-quick time. The oyster sauce adds a gloss and sophistication to these simple vegetables.

4 **garlic** cloves, sliced

1-inch piece fresh **ginger**, peeled and cut into matchsticks

½ **onion**, finely sliced

¼ pound **baby corn**, cut in half at an angle

¼ pound **sugar snap peas**

1 tablespoon **oyster sauce**

1 tablespoon **fish sauce**

1 tablespoon boiling **water**

2 tablespoons **sunflower oil**

freshly ground **black pepper**

1 **ASSEMBLE** all the prepared vegetables next to the stove.

2 **BLEND** the oyster and fish sauces with the water in a bowl.

3 **HEAT** a wok before adding the oil. Allow to become hot, then toss in the garlic, ginger, and onion, turning all the time so that the garlic does not brown and become bitter.

4 **ADD** the baby corn and sugar snap peas, and toss well 2 minutes, then pour in the sauce mixture. Cover with a lid and cook 1 minute.

5 **TOP** with a little black pepper and serve on a warm serving dish.

MIXED STIR-FRY VEGETABLES

PAD PAK RUAM MITR

SERVES **4**   PREPARATION TIME: **12** MINUTES   COOKING TIME: **5** MINUTES

This deliciously crisp and colorful stir-fry makes the perfect accompaniment to any main dish, or could just be eaten on its own. Choose any vegetables you want, but aim for a good mix of color and texture for the perfect result.

---

1 pound **mixed vegetables**: broccoli, string beans, Brussels sprouts, carrots, cabbage, bean sprouts, and/or spinach (any combination), trimmed and cut into bite-size pieces

3 tablespoons **water**

2 tablespoons **fish sauce**

2 tablespoons **oyster sauce**

3 tablespoons **sunflower oil**

2 **garlic** cloves, finely chopped

½ teaspoon **sugar**

freshly ground **black pepper**

1 **RINSE** and drain the vegetables. Set the cabbage, bean sprouts, and/or spinach aside. Assemble all the vegetables by the stove.

2 **COMBINE** the water, fish sauce, and oyster sauce in a small bowl.

3 **HEAT** a wok, add the oil, and first fry the garlic without browning it too much.

4 **ADD** all the remaining vegetables, except for the cabbage, bean sprouts, and/or spinach, then add the sugar and season with black pepper. Toss well, turning all the time to cook while retaining the crunchiness.

5 **ADD** the sauce mixture and the remaining vegetables. Reduce the heat, cover, and cook a further 2 minutes.

6 **SERVE** on a warm serving dish.

STIR-FRY BROCCOLI AND CARROTS WITH BEAN CURD AND PEANUTS

PAD BROC-CO-LI KAB TOFU

**SERVES 4   PREPARATION TIME: 8–10 MINUTES
COOKING TIME: 6 MINUTES**

A simple vegetable dish is transformed into a vegetarian main meal with the addition of some deep-fried bean curd and some lightly crushed peanuts.

---

2 **carrots**, trimmed

⅔ pound **broccoli**, any tender stems cut into matchsticks, head divided into flowerets

1 tablespoon **fish sauce**

1 tablespoon **oyster sauce**

4 tablespoons hot **water**, or **chicken** or **vegetable stock** (*see page 23*)

3 tablespoons **sunflower oil**

1 **onion**, cut into fine wedges

1-inch piece fresh **ginger**, peeled and cut into matchsticks

freshly ground **black pepper**

¼ pound cubes **fried bean curd** (optional)

scant ¼ cup roasted **peanuts**, lightly crushed (optional)

1 **LAY** the carrots on a chopping board and make an angled cut along the length of each one, then another cut very close to make a "V" shape. Remove the strip and repeat the process two or three times around each carrot, then slice the carrots finely to make pretty flower shapes.

2 **PLUNGE** the broccoli into a saucepan of boiling water 1 minute to turn it bright green. Drain immediately and rinse with cold water.

3 **BLEND** the fish and oyster sauces with water or stock and set aside.

4 **HEAT** a wok and warm the oil. Fry the onion and ginger first without browning, then toss in the carrots, and stir-fry over high heat 2 minutes. Add any tender broccoli stems and the flowerets. Keep turning over high heat 1 minute.

5 **POUR** in the sauce mixture and add some black pepper. Cover with a lid and steam 1 minute. Add the bean curd at this stage, if using.

6 **SERVE** immediately, topped with the peanuts, if using.

SPICY STRING BEANS

PAD PED TOU KAG

SERVES 4   PREPARATION TIME: 6—8 MINUTES   COOKING TIME: 5 MINUTES

*These beans are a rich vibrant color and full of flavor and crispness.
The combination of the beans with aromatic curry paste and piquant
fish sauce creates a perfect vegetable dish for any Thai meal.*

1 pound **string** or **long beans**, stalk end trimmed, and sliced into 2-inch pieces

3 tablespoons **sunflower oil**

1 tablespoon **red curry paste** *(see page 24)*

2 tablespoons **fish sauce**

2 tablespoons **sugar**

½ cup boiling **water**

1 **PLUNGE** the string beans into a saucepan of boiling water 30 seconds, then drain, and set aside.

2 **HEAT** a wok, add the oil, and swirl it over the surface of the pan. Add the curry paste, then fry over moderate heat until it changes color and gives off a rich, fragrant aroma.

3 **ADD** the string beans and stir-fry until they are tender. Add the fish sauce, sugar, and water and bring the mixture rapidly to a boil.

4 **TRANSFER** the cooked beans and sauce to a warm serving bowl and serve immediately.

MARKET SALAD *SOM TAM*

SERVES 4   PREPARATION TIME: 15–20 MINUTES

A traditional salad of coarsely grated green papaya and tomato wedges mixed with long beans, fresh red chili, lemon or lime juice, fish sauce, and pounded dried shrimp. If green papaya is unavailable, use white cabbage or carrot.

---

1 pound **green papaya**, peeled, or **white cabbage**, shredded, and **carrot**, grated (optional)

1 **red chili**, seeded and sliced

1–2 **long beans**, sliced, or 6 **string beans**

1 teaspoon **sugar**

4 tablespoons **fish sauce**

juice of 1 **lemon** or **lime**

1 ounce **dried shrimp**, pounded to a powder using a mortar and pestle

2 **tomatoes**, cut into eighths, or 8 **cherry tomatoes**, cut in half

¼–⅓ cup **peanuts**, crushed to garnish

1–2 handfuls **cilantro leaves**, chopped to garnish

1 **HOLD** the papaya in one hand and make deep, slim cuts down into the flesh on one side with a very sharp knife. Then take off thin slices lengthwise, leaving you with consistently sized shreds. Repeat all the way around on the other side.

2 **CRUSH** the chili lightly with the beans and sugar using a mortar and pestle, then add the fish sauce and lemon or lime juice to taste.

3 **PLACE** the powdered dried shrimp, tomatoes, papaya or cabbage (or a mixture of cabbage and carrot) in a bowl, add the crushed chili mixture, and toss lightly.

4 **PLACE** on a serving dish. Top with the peanuts and cilantro leaves just before serving.

GREEN MANGO SALAD

YUM MA-MAUNG

**SERVES 4   PREPARATION TIME: 15 MINUTES
COOKING TIME: 1–2 MINUTES**

A stunning layered salad of tart green mangoes, dried shrimp, toasted coconut, and finely sliced red onion, on a lettuce-lined dish, drizzled with a spicy sweet and sour dressing, and garnished with mint or cilantro leaves.

2 large **green mangoes** or hard unripe **yellow mangoes** (these will give a sweeter result), or 1 **pomelo** or **grapefruit**

½ cup **dried coconut (unsweetened)**

head of soft **lettuce**

2 ounces **dried shrimp**, pounded to a powder using a mortar and pestle

1 **red onion**, finely sliced

mint leaves, torn, or **cilantro leaves**

DRESSING:

juice of 1 large **lime** or ½ **lemon**

3 tablespoons **fish sauce**

1–2 **bird's eye chilies** (or more), seeded and finely sliced

2 tablespoons **dark brown sugar**

1 **PEEL** the mangoes with a vegetable peeler. Holding one in the palm of your hand, use a sharp knife to make lots of close cuts in the flesh of the mango. Now slice through the close cuts to make fine shards of flesh and repeat on the other side. Repeat with the second mango. If using a pomelo or grapefruit, remove the skin, divide into segments, and remove the membranes, then chop lightly.

2 **WARM** a skillet, then dry-fry the coconut 1–2 minutes until golden, keeping it on the move to prevent it burning.

3 **BLEND** together the dressing ingredients in a cup.

4 **LINE** a serving dish with lettuce leaves, then layer up the mango, powdered shrimp, coconut and onion, and some of the cilantro or torn mint leaves.

5 **POUR** the dressing over the salad and garnish with the remaining cilantro or torn mint. Toss before each person takes their helping.

THAI MUSSAMAN CURRY

GAENG MUSSAMAN

SERVES 6   PREPARATION TIME: 25 MINUTES   COOKING TIME: 2½ HOURS

The tamarind juice adds contrasting sharpness in this hearty combination of spices, beef, nuts, shallots, and potatoes. The spices in the Mussaman curry paste indicate the influence of Indian and Arab traders from centuries ago.

2½ cups canned **coconut milk**

1⅓ cups **water**

2¼ pounds good quality chuck **steak**, trimmed and cut into 1-inch cubes

2 tablespoons **tamarind pulp**

⅔ cup warm **water**

4 tablespoons **Mussaman curry paste** (*see page 25*)

⅔ pound tiny **new potatoes**, cut in half if larger than bite size

½ pound small **onions** or **shallots**

3 tablespoons **sunflower oil**

⅓ cup **roasted peanuts**

¼ cup **dark brown** or **palm sugar**

juice of ½ **lemon** or **lime**

1 **red chili**, sliced to garnish

1 RINSE a casserole or heavy-based saucepan with water—this helps to prevent the base of the pan sticking during the slow cooking. Pour in the coconut milk and water and slowly bring to a boil.

2 STIR in the beef, return to a boil, then turn the heat down and simmer gently, uncovered, 1½ hours, or until the beef is tender. Meanwhile, soak the tamarind pulp in the warm water 10 minutes, then strain (see page 20).

3 LIFT the meat out with a slotted spoon into a separate container and reserve.

4 REDUCE the liquid in the pan by boiling 5 minutes. Add the curry paste and cook 3–4 minutes, stirring, to bring out the flavors.

5 FRY the potatoes and onions in hot oil in a separate skillet 5 minutes until golden. Add to the spicy coconut sauce with the meat and the peanuts, and cook 20–30 minutes.

6 ADD the strained tamarind juice, sugar, and lemon or lime juice. Cook a further 10 minutes before serving garnished with the sliced chili. (Ideally, cook this the day before you need it, to let the flavors develop, and reheat 1–1½ hours at 325°F in a covered dish.)

JUNGLE CURRY *GAENG PAH*

SERVES 4   PREPARATION TIME: **25** MINUTES   COOKING TIME: **1¾** HOURS

A rustic meal artfully cooked so that the beef is beautifully tender but the vegetables retain their natural crispness. This curry is so-called because the itinerant cook would have used whatever could be found to prepare the meal.

3 tablespoons **sunflower oil**

3 tablespoons **red curry paste** *(see page 24)*

1½ pounds chuck **steak**, cut into thin, even-size strips across the grain

3 tablespoons **fish sauce**

3 pieces **krachai**, cut into matchsticks

⅓ pound **long** or **string beans**, cut into 1-inch lengths

⅓ pound egg-sized **white eggplants**, cut into quarters

¼ pound **baby corn**, halved if liked

3 **lime leaves**, torn

1 teaspoon fresh **green peppercorns**

2–3 **green chilies**, seeded, if liked, and sliced

2 **sweet basil** sprigs, leaves only

3 cups well-flavored **beef stock** or 1¼ cups canned **beef consommé** made up with 1¾ cups **water**

2 teaspoons **sugar**

1 **HEAT** a wok and then add the oil. When hot, add the curry paste to taste and stir until it releases a rich aroma.

2 **ADD** the slices of beef and stir constantly until the meat changes color. Add the fish sauce, then the krachai, vegetables, lime leaves, peppercorns, chilies, and some of the basil leaves.

3 **STIR** in the stock and sugar and bring to a boil. Half cover and simmer gently 1–1½ hours, or until the beef is tender. Taste for seasoning and adjust if necessary. Garnish with the remaining basil leaves and serve.

NORTHERN THAI CURRY WITH PORK AND GINGER *GAENG HUNG LAY*

SERVES 4–6   PREPARATION TIME: 30 MINUTES, PLUS 1¼ HOURS
SOAKING AND MARINATING TIME   COOKING TIME: 1¼ HOURS

A typical earthy flavored pork curry made using Hung Lay curry paste, sharp tamarind juice, turmeric, fish sauce, and ginger, and garnished with pork crackling.

1 tablespoon **tamarind pulp**

1½ pounds **pork**, trimmed and cut into large pieces

3 tablespoons **Hung Lay curry paste** (*see page 25*)

2 teaspoons **ground turmeric**

1 teaspoon **five spice powder**

2 tablespoons **brown** or **palm sugar**

3 tablespoons **fish sauce**

3-inch piece fresh **ginger**, peeled and cut into matchsticks

3 **shallots**, sliced

4 **garlic** cloves, crushed

3 cups **chicken stock** (*see page 23*)

1½ ounces **pork crackling** (sold as *chicaron*) to garnish

1 SOAK the tamarind pulp in 4 tablespoons warm water 15 minutes, then strain (see page 20).

2 COMBINE the pork with the curry paste, turmeric, five spice powder, sugar, strained tamarind juice, fish sauce, one-third of the ginger, the shallots, and garlic.

3 MIX well, then cover, and let marinate in a cool place 1 hour.

4 WARM a casserole or wok. Add the marinated pork and stock. Allow to come to a boil, then reduce the heat to a simmer. Cover with the lid just slightly off center and simmer on low heat 1¼ hours, or until the pork becomes tender.

5 GARNISH with pork crackling and the remaining ginger.

GREEN CHICKEN CURRY

GAENG KHIEW WAAN GAI

**SERVES 4   PREPARATION TIME: 15 MINUTES
COOKING TIME: 12–15 MINUTES**

*A huge favorite, almost the signature dish of Thai restaurants everywhere.
Here slices of chicken breast are cooked in the green curry paste and coconut
sauce, with torn lime leaves and fish sauce.*

1⅔ cups canned **coconut milk**

3 tablespoons **green curry paste** *(see page 24)*

2 boneless **chicken** breasts (6–7 ounces each),
   cut into even-size strips

⅔ cup **water** or **stock**

2–3 tablespoons **fish sauce**

1 teaspoon **sugar**

4–5 **lime leaves**, torn or finely shredded

¼ pound tiny **pea eggplants**, stalks removed

1 small handful **cilantro leaves**,
   roughly chopped

1–2 **sweet basil** sprigs, leaves only to garnish

1 small **green** and/or **red chili**, seeded and cut
   into strips to garnish

1 **POUR** one-third of the coconut milk into a heated wok. Let it begin to
bubble around the edges.

2 **STIR** in the curry paste and stir-fry 2–3 minutes, stirring frequently,
to bring out the full flavor.

3 **ADD** the chicken strips, keeping them separate. Turn them in the
sauce in the wok until they are well coated.

4 **MIX** the remaining coconut milk with the water or stock plus
2 tablespoons of the fish sauce and the sugar and add to the wok.
Finally, add the lime leaves, eggplants, and cilantro leaves.

5 **SIMMER** 10 minutes, or until the chicken pieces are tender. Taste and
add more fish sauce if liked.

6 **TRANSFER** to a warm serving bowl and garnish with the basil leaves
and strips of green or red chilies, or both.

ROAST DUCK CURRY *GAENG PHED PED YANG*

**SERVES 4—6   PREPARATION TIME: 10 MINUTES
COOKING TIME: 50 MINUTES, PLUS ROASTING TIME**

Delicious morsels of roast duck and crunchy, tart, pea eggplants are added to this curry sauce, which is based on the famous green curry paste and coconut milk combination, to make one of the most famous of all Thai curries.

1 **duck** (5 pounds) or 2 good-sized **duck** breast portions

1⅔ cups canned **coconut milk**

1–2 tablespoons **green curry paste** (see page 24)

4 **lime leaves**, torn

2 tablespoons **fish sauce**

1¼ cups **stock** or **water**

1 large **red** and 1 large **green chili**, seeded and sliced

½ pound **pea eggplants**, stalks removed

3 **tomatoes**, quartered

2 **sweet basil** sprigs and **cilantro** stems, leaves only

1 **ROAST** the duck as suggested on the packaging. Allow to cool, then cut into small pieces, discarding the backbone, any fat, and other bony pieces. Set aside. Alternatively, pan-fry or roast two duck breasts as suggested on the packaging. Allow to cool, then slice finely.

2 **HEAT** a wok, then pour in one-third of the coconut milk and heat until bubbling. Add the curry paste and stir over moderate heat until the mixture gives off a rich aroma.

3 **REDUCE** the heat and add the torn lime leaves and fish sauce to taste, then stir in the duck meat, and turn in the sauce until it is all thoroughly coated with the spicy mixture.

4 **BLEND** the remaining coconut milk with the stock or water and add to the curry. Stir, then add the chilies and pea eggplants.

5 **COOK** 30 minutes, then add the tomatoes, some of the basil leaves, and all the cilantro leaves. Bubble gently a further 10 minutes, then serve, garnished with the remaining basil.

RED CHICKEN CURRY

GAENG PHED GAI

**SERVES 4   PREPARATION TIME: 20 MINUTES
COOKING TIME: 45–50 MINUTES**

*Small chicken joints blended with red curry paste, coconut milk, and a dash or
two of fish sauce. The whole dish is enhanced with crunchy bamboo shoots
or earthy straw mushrooms and sweet basil leaves.*

1⅔ cups canned **coconut milk**

3 tablespoons **red curry paste** *(see page 24)*

3-pound **chicken**, jointed and each quarter
divided into 2 or 4 portions, or 2–3 boneless
chicken breasts (6 ounces each), cut
into strips.

4–5 **lime leaves**, torn or finely shredded

⅔ cup **water**

2–3 tablespoons **fish sauce**

1 teaspoon **sugar**

1 can sliced **bamboo shoots** (9 ounces) or
straw mushrooms (14 ounces), drained

1–2 **sweet basil** sprigs, leaves only

1 **red chili**, seeded and finely sliced
to garnish

1 **HEAT** a wok, then pour in one-third of the coconut milk and heat
until bubbling. Add the curry paste and stir-fry 2–3 minutes over
moderate heat to bring out the flavor.

2 **ADD** the chicken portions or strips. Turn them in the sauce in the wok
until they are well coated.

3 **MIX** the remaining coconut milk with the water plus 2 tablespoons of
the fish sauce and the sugar, and add to the wok. Finally, add the lime
leaves and bamboo shoots or straw mushrooms.

4 **SIMMER** 40–45 minutes if using chicken portions, or until they are
tender. Simmer only 10 minutes if using chicken strips. Taste, and add
more fish sauce if liked, and most of the basil.

5 **TRANSFER** to a warm serving bowl and garnish with the remaining
basil and the red chili.

SHRIMP AND PINEAPPLE CURRY

GAENG KHAU GOONG

SERVES **4**   PREPARATION TIME: **12–15** MINUTES,
PLUS **10** MINUTES SOAKING TIME   COOKING TIME: **12–15** MINUTES

Shrimp take on a new identity when simmered in coconut milk and red curry paste, hot with chili, sweet and juicy with fresh pineapple, salty with powdered dried shrimp, and sharpened with tamarind juice—all the essential Thai flavors.

1 teaspoon **tamarind pulp**

1⅔ cups canned **coconut milk**

2 tablespoons **red curry paste** (*see page 24*)

⅔ cup warm **water**

1 **red** and 1 **green bird's eye chili**, seeded and sliced

1 tablespoon **dried shrimp**, pounded to a powder using a mortar and pestle

2 tablespoons **fish sauce**

1 pound shelled **tiger shrimp** or same weight **white fish** or **salmon**, skinned, boned, and cut into bite-size pieces

6–8 **cherry tomatoes**, halved if liked

1 thick slice fresh or canned **pineapple**, cut into small pieces

1 **basil** sprig, leaves only

1 SOAK the tamarind pulp in 3 tablespoons warm water 10 minutes, then strain (see page 20).

2 HEAT a wok, then pour in one-third of the coconut milk, and heat until bubbling. Add the curry paste and stir over moderate heat to bring out the flavor.

3 ADD the remaining coconut milk plus the warm water, chilies, powdered shrimp, fish sauce, and strained tamarind juice. Bring slowly to a boil, then simmer 8–10 minutes.

4 ADD the shrimp, or fish if using, tomatoes, and pineapple. Cook gently 3–4 minutes, then add most of the basil leaves at the last moment.

5 TRANSFER to a warm bowl and scatter with the remaining basil.

KHUN NAN'S STEAMED FISH CURRY *HOR MOK PLA*

SERVES 4   PREPARATION TIME: 20 MINUTES   COOKING TIME: 15 MINUTES

Traditionally this curry would have been cooked in a banana leaf cup,
which does add a special flavor and looks sensational too.

1⅔ cups canned **coconut milk**

2 tablespoons **red curry paste** *(see page 24)*

2 tablespoons **fish sauce**

1 **egg**, beaten

¼ cup **rice flour**

1 teaspoon **sugar**

1 pound **cod**, **haddock** or **salmon** steak
or other fish of your choice, skinned and cut
into bite-size pieces, or raw **tiger shrimp**,
cut in half

6 **lime leaves**, very finely shredded

2 teaspoons **sunflower oil** (optional)

4 **banana cups** (optional)

2 **Chinese cabbage** leaves, torn into pieces

2 **sweet basil** sprigs, leaves only, torn

1 **red chili**, sliced

1 **PUT** the coconut milk (reserving 2 tablespoons for the garnish), curry paste, fish sauce, beaten egg, rice flour, and sugar in a bowl and blend to a smooth thick batter. Add the fish pieces and four of the lime leaves, reserving the rest for the garnish.

2 **BRUSH** four large ramekins lightly with oil or make four banana cups, if using (see page 26).

3 **PLACE** a piece of Chinese cabbage in the base of each ramekin. Divide the fish mixture between them and top with the torn basil leaves and some of the slices of chili.

4 **PLACE** the ramekins in a large, wide skillet with boiling water to come halfway up their sides. Cover and steam 15 minutes until the tops are just set (a skewer will come out clean). Alternatively, steam for the same time on a large bamboo steaming tray set over a wok and covered; cook in a water bath in the microwave on full power, covered loosely with plastic wrap (8 minutes cooking time and 2 minutes resting); or cook in an electric steamer 15 minutes. If using banana cups, fill at the last minute to avoid any possibility of leaking and use crumpled foil to keep the cups steady.

5 **SERVE** hot, garnished with the reserved coconut milk, reserved shredded lime leaves, and reserved chili slices.

MIXED VEGETABLE CURRY

GAENG KARI PAK

SERVES **4–6**   PREPARATION TIME: **20** MINUTES
COOKING TIME: **12–15** MINUTES

Perfectly prepared vegetables, gently cooked in coconut milk and combined with curry paste. Use baby corn, white eggplants cut into quarters, carrots cut into fine slices or batons, and zucchini either sliced or cut into neat chunks.

1⅔ cups canned **coconut milk**

2 tablespoons **red** or **green curry paste**
(*see page 24*)

¾-inch piece **turmeric root** or 2 teaspoons **ground turmeric**

1¾ cups **vegetable stock** (*see page 23*)

1⅓ pounds **vegetables**: baby corn, halved, white eggplants, quartered, carrots, cut into batons, and zucchini, sliced

2 tablespoons **fish sauce**

3 **lime leaves**, finely shredded

1 **basil** sprig and 1 **cilantro stem**, leaves only

1 **HEAT** a wok, then pour in one-third of the coconut milk and heat until bubbling. Add the curry paste and stir over moderate heat to bring out the flavor.

2 **PEEL** the piece of turmeric, if using, wearing gloves to protect against staining, then pound it to a paste using a mortar and pestle. Add this or the ground turmeric to the wok along with the remaining coconut milk and vegetable stock, then bring to a boil.

3 **ADD** the prepared vegetables, return to a gentle boil, stirring all the time. Add the fish sauce and some of the lime, basil, and cilantro leaves.

4 **SIMMER** gently, testing a piece of vegetable now and then, until the vegetables are just cooked but the baby corn and carrots are still slightly crunchy. Taste and adjust the seasoning, adding more fish sauce if wanted.

5 **SERVE** in a hot bowl, garnished with the remaining leaves.

BEEF WITH BROCCOLI AND OYSTER SAUCE

NEAU PAD PAK NAMMAUN HOY

SERVES 4   PREPARATION TIME: 10 MINUTES
COOKING TIME: 7–8 MINUTES

*The tenderest filet mignon and the brightest green broccoli make perfect
partners. Add a dash of oyster sauce, some garlic, scallions, and a generous
amount of seasoning and you have a stunning creation.*

½ pound **broccoli**, cut into tiny flowerets

1 pound **filet mignon**, sliced into neat,
even-size pieces

2 **garlic** cloves, crushed

2 tablespoons **oyster sauce**

5 tablespoons **chicken stock** (*see page 23*)

salt and freshly ground **black pepper**

5 **scallions**, cut into short lengths

4 tablespoons **sunflower oil**

1 **ASSEMBLE** all the ingredients.

2 **PLUNGE** the broccoli flowerets into boiling water 1 minute, then
drain, and rinse with cold water.

3 **HEAT** a wok, add the oil, and, when very hot, toss in the beef and garlic.
Stir-fry 4 minutes until the meat has changed color and looks tender.

4 **ADD** the blanched broccoli flowerets, oyster sauce, and the stock.
Cover and cook over high heat 1–2 minutes, stirring once or twice.

5 **TASTE** for seasoning, toss in the scallions, and stir-fry a further
few seconds.

6 **SERVE** immediately in a hot serving dish.

STIR-FRY NOODLES WITH PORK OR BEEF

GUAY TIEW PAD SI-EW

SERVES **4**   PREPARATION TIME: **10** MINUTES
COOKING TIME: **6—8** MINUTES

Rice noodles tossed with stir-fried tender pork or filet mignon, Chinese leaves, and delicately scrambled egg, all enhanced with soy and crushed yellow bean sauces and a handful of scallions—an unbelievable gastronomic experience.

1 pound **rice noodles** (*guay tiew*)

2 **garlic** cloves, crushed

½ pound lean **pork** or **filet mignon**, cut into thin strips

1 large **egg**, beaten

6 **Chinese leaves** or any **green leaves**, trimmed and chopped into bite-size pieces

1 teaspoon **dark soy sauce**

1 tablespoon **light soy sauce**

1 tablespoon **crushed yellow bean sauce**

1 teaspoon **sugar**

salt and freshly ground **black pepper**

4 **scallions**, cut into neat lengths

2 tablespoons **sunflower oil**

1 SEPARATE the noodles and plunge into boiling water. Drain, then slice the folded noodles into ribbons.

2 ASSEMBLE the remaining ingredients.

3 HEAT a wok, add the oil, and, when hot, fry the garlic until turning golden, then add the beef or pork, and toss all the time until the meat changes color and is cooked. This will take just a couple of minutes for beef and a little longer for pork.

4 ADD the egg to the wok and stir until it just begins to scramble, then add the Chinese or other leaves. Cook only a few seconds, then add the rice noodles.

5 TOSS well and then add the soy sauces, crushed yellow bean sauce, and sugar. Mix well and taste for seasoning. Add most of the scallions.

6 PLACE in a warm serving bowl and garnish with the remaining scallions. Serve immediately.

STIR-FRY PORK AND SHRIMP WITH WING BEANS *MOO LAE GOONG PAD TAO*

SERVES 4   PREPARATION TIME: 8–10 MINUTES
COOKING TIME: 10 MINUTES

A fabulous mixture of tender pork tossed in a red curry paste with bright green wing beans and fresh shrimp moistened with fish sauce and sweetened to just the right degree.

½ pound **wing** or **string beans**, cut into 1-inch lengths

2 tablespoons **red curry paste** (*see page 24*)

½ pound boneless **pork**, thinly sliced

3–4 tablespoons hot **water**

4 tablespoons **fish sauce**

½ cup shelled cooked **shrimp**

1 tablespoon **light brown sugar**

4 tablespoons **sunflower oil**

freshly ground **black pepper**

1 PLUNGE the beans into boiling water 2 minutes, then drain, rinse with cold water, and drain again.

2 ASSEMBLE the remaining ingredients.

3 HEAT a wok, add the oil, and, when hot, stir-fry the curry paste to bring out the flavor. Add the pork slices and cook until the pork changes color. Thin slices will cook quite quickly.

4 ADD the hot water, fish sauce, shrimp, and beans. Stir well, then add the sugar and black pepper. Taste, and adjust the seasoning, then serve at once.

STIR-FRY CHILI PORK

MOO PAD PRIK

SERVES 4   PREPARATION TIME: 10 MINUTES   COOKING TIME: 8 MINUTES

A quick and sumptuous dish of thinly sliced boneless pork, tossed with garlic, chili, and scallions, moistened with Thai fish sauce, and served piping hot. It is important that the pork is sliced very thinly so that it will cook quickly.

1 pound boneless **pork**, trimmed and sliced into neat, even-size pieces

1 small **onion**, finely sliced

2 **garlic** cloves, crushed

1–2 **red chilies**, seeded and finely sliced

4 **scallions**, cut into short lengths

4 tablespoons **stock** or **water**

1 tablespoon **fish sauce**

4 tablespoons **sunflower oil**

freshly ground **black pepper**

1 **ASSEMBLE** all the ingredients.

2 **HEAT** a wok, add the oil, and, when hot, toss in the pork, onion, and garlic. Stir-fry 5–6 minutes until the pork changes color and is tender.

3 **ADD** the remaining ingredients and quickly toss together. Taste for seasoning and serve immediately on a hot dish.

STIR-FRY CHICKEN WITH BASIL LEAVES

GAI PAD BAI KAPROW

SERVES 4   **PREPARATION TIME: 12–15** MINUTES
COOKING TIME: 8 MINUTES

The chicken is wonderfully perfumed with fresh basil leaves, but the bird's eye chilies add dragon-like fire. To be truly authentic, the fiendishly hot chilies should be simply crushed, but you may prefer to remove some of the seeds.

1 small, finger-long red **chili** to garnish

2 **chicken** breasts (6–7 ounces each), boned and skinned and cut into neat, bite-size pieces

2 **garlic** cloves, crushed

1 **onion**, finely sliced

15 **holy basil leaves**

2–3 **bird's eye chilies**, seeded, if liked, and sliced or crushed

2 tablespoons **fish sauce**

1 teaspoon **light brown sugar**

4 tablespoons **sunflower oil**

1 **MAKE** a chili flower following the instructions on page 26, leaving it to soak in ice water while you prepare and cook the stir-fry.

2 **ASSEMBLE** all the ingredients.

3 **HEAT** a wok, add half the oil, and, when hot, stir-fry the chicken pieces and garlic together. Stir-fry until the chicken pieces change color and are cooked through. Remove from the wok and keep warm.

4 **WIPE** the wok with paper towels, then add the remaining oil, and stir-fry the onion with most of the basil leaves and chilies 3 minutes.

5 **RETURN** the chicken to the wok, add the fish sauce and sugar, and mix well.

6 **PLACE** in a hot serving dish and garnish with the chili flower and remaining basil leaves. Serve at once.

STIR-FRY DUCK BREASTS WITH GINGER AND BLACK BEAN SAUCE *PED PAD KHING*

SERVES 4   PREPARATION TIME: 15 MINUTES
COOKING TIME: 8 MINUTES, PLUS 1 HOUR RENDERING TIME

Another winning combination—fresh ginger, black bean sauce, garlic, and Chinese mushrooms stir-fried with juicy slices of duck breast and scallions, and served garnished with shreds of crispy duck skin.

2 boneless **duck** breasts (10–11 ounces each), finely sliced

6 **Chinese mushrooms**

1 **garlic** clove, crushed

1-inch piece fresh **ginger**, peeled and shredded

1 small **onion**, sliced

1–2 tablespoons **black bean sauce**

1 teaspoon **sugar**

freshly ground **black pepper**

4 **scallions**, cut into short lengths

3 tablespoons **sunflower oil** or **duck fat** (optional)

1 **HEAT** the oven to 350°F.

2 **TRIM** the skin from the duck breasts, if liked, and render down in an ovenproof dish in the oven about 1 hour until all the fat has melted and the skin is crisp. Reserve the duck fat for cooking the meat, if wanted, and slice the crisp skin into fine strips for the garnish. Meanwhile, soak the Chinese mushrooms in warm water 20–30 minutes.

3 **ASSEMBLE** all the remaining ingredients.

4 **DRAIN** the mushrooms, reserving 2–3 tablespoons of the soaking liquid. Discard the stems and slice the mushroom caps finely.

5 **HEAT** the oil or duck fat in a wok and, when hot, add the duck slices, garlic, and ginger, and toss constantly until the duck meat changes color and is tender.

6 **ADD** the onion, mushrooms, black bean sauce, sugar, and the mushroom soaking liquid. Toss well and taste for seasoning.

7 **ADD** the scallions and turn out immediately on to a hot serving dish. Serve scattered with the crispy skin slices, if liked.

STIR-FRY CHICKEN WITH CASHEW NUTS

GAI PAD MAMAUNG HIMMAPARN

**SERVES 4   PREPARATION TIME: 12–15 MINUTES
COOKING TIME: 6 MINUTES**

A favorite combination of sweet, almost creamy, cashews roasted to bring out their nuttiness and stir-fried with the tenderest chicken breasts, subtly flavored with fish and oyster sauces and just a hint of garlic.

---

2 skinless **chicken** breasts (½ pound each), sliced into neat, even-size strips

1 **garlic** clove, crushed

1 **onion**, finely sliced

generous ⅓ cup roasted **cashew nuts**, halved lengthwise

3 tablespoons **fish sauce**

1 tablespoon **oyster sauce**

4 **scallions**, cut into short lengths

salt and freshly ground **black pepper**

3 tablespoons **sunflower oil**

1 **ASSEMBLE** all the ingredients.

2 **HEAT** a wok, add the oil, and, when hot, toss in the chicken and garlic, and stir-fry 3–4 minutes until the chicken pieces are tender and golden.

3 **ADD** the remaining ingredients. Cook only 1 minute, then taste for seasoning, and serve on a hot serving dish.

SWEET AND SOUR CHICKEN

PAD PRIEW-WAAN GAI

SERVES 4   PREPARATION TIME: 15 MINUTES
COOKING TIME: 8–10 MINUTES

Nothing like Chinese sweet and sour dishes, here the chicken is stir-fried gently, then simmered with colorful red and green vegetables, flavored with tomato, sharpened with rice vinegar, and sweetened with sugar to form a rich-tasting sauce.

2 skinless **chicken** breasts (½ pound each), sliced into neat, even-size strips

¼ small **onion**, finely sliced

¼ each **red** and **green pepper**, finely sliced

1-inch piece **cucumber**, finely sliced

4 **cherry tomatoes**, halved

4 **scallions**, cut into short lengths

1 teaspoon **tomato paste**

1 tablespoon **rice vinegar**

1 tablespoon **fish sauce**

1 teaspoon **sugar**

4 tablespoons **chicken stock** (*see page 23*) (*optional*)

4 tablespoons **sunflower oil**

freshly ground **black pepper**

cilantro leaves to garnish

1 ASSEMBLE all the ingredients.

2 HEAT a wok, add the oil, and, when hot, stir-fry the chicken pieces 3–5 minutes until they change color and are tender.

3 ADD all the other ingredients along with the stock, if needed, to make a sauce. Cook 3–4 minutes. Taste, and adjust the seasoning.

4 SERVE on a warm dish garnished with cilantro leaves.

STIR-FRY SQUID WITH GARLIC

PLA MEUK KRATIEM PRIKTHAI

SERVES 4   PREPARATION TIME: 20 MINUTES   COOKING TIME: 5 MINUTES

As the attractively prepared squid is stir-fried with garlic, cilantro, freshly ground black pepper, and oyster sauce, the juices give off a heady aroma.

1 pound ready-cleaned **squid**

2 tablespoons **sunflower oil**

1–2 **garlic** cloves, crushed

2 **cilantro** stems, stalks pounded

½ teaspoon freshly ground **black pepper**

1 tablespoon **oyster sauce**

6 **scallions**, cut into 1-inch lengths

1 **PREPARE** the squid and cut any tiny squid into rings and the larger ones into strips (see page 19). Do not discard the tentacles, which are usually tucked into each ready-cleaned squid—add them to the recipe.

2 **ASSEMBLE** all the ingredients.

3 **HEAT** a wok, add the oil, and, when hot, quickly fry the garlic and pounded cilantro stalks (reserving the leaves for the garnish) to bring out the flavor.

4 **KEEP** the wok over high heat, then add the squid and tentacles. Stir-fry quickly 2–3 minutes.

5 **ADD** the pepper and oyster sauce, and finally the scallions.

6 **PLACE** on a hot serving dish and serve garnished with the reserved cilantro leaves.

STIR-FRY SCALLOPS WITH CHILI AND BASIL LEAVES *HOY SHELL PAD BAI KAPROW*

SERVES 3–4   PREPARATION TIME: 10 MINUTES
COOKING TIME: 2–3 MINUTES

Scallops stir-fried with onion, chili, basil, and fish sauce create a sensational dish. Scallops are best cooked briefly, and so are highly suited to a stir-fry.

6–8 large **scallops**

½ **onion**, finely sliced

1 large **red** or **green chili**, seeded and finely sliced

2 **holy basil** sprigs, leaves only

4 **scallions**, cut into short lengths

2 tablespoons **fish sauce**

1 teaspoon **sugar**

freshly ground **black pepper**

3 tablespoons **sunflower oil**

1 **CUT** the scallops horizontally through the center to make two even-size round shapes. Place on paper towels to drain any excess moisture.

2 **ASSEMBLE** all the other ingredients. When ready to cook, heat a wok, add the oil, and, when hot, toss in the scallops and stir-fry 1 minute.

3 **PUSH** the scallops to one side, then add the onion to the wok with the chili and basil leaves. Keep tossing, then add the scallions, fish sauce, sugar, and pepper.

4 **TASTE** and adjust the seasoning, then serve immediately on a hot serving dish.

STIR-FRY GREEN VEGETABLES WITH YELLOW BEAN SAUCE *PAT PAK BOONG FAI DAENG*

SERVES 4   PREPARATION TIME: 5 MINUTES   COOKING TIME: 3—4 MINUTES

Oriental greens stir-fried with a glorious mixture of crushed yellow bean sauce, garlic, and chilies. If you cannot buy pak boong, baby spinach makes a perfect substitute. Alternatively, use a combination of pak choy and Savoy cabbage.

1–2 **chilies**, seeded and finely chopped

3 tablespoons **crushed yellow bean sauce**

1 **garlic** clove, crushed

1 tablespoon **sugar**

3 tablespoons **sunflower oil**

1 pound **pak boong** or **young spinach**, or **pak choy**, leaves used whole and white stalks cut into bite-size pieces, and **Savoy cabbage**, leaves torn

1 PLACE the chopped chilies, crushed yellow bean sauce, garlic, and sugar in a bowl.

2 HEAT a wok, add the oil, and, when hot, toss in the spicy sauce and the green vegetables together. Stir-fry 3–4 minutes.

3 PLACE on a hot plate and serve at once.

STIR-FRY LONG BEANS, TOMATOES, AND CHINESE LEAVES

PAD TUR FAK YAO, MAKEUR THED KAB KANA

SERVES 4   PREPARATION TIME: 8 MINUTES   COOKING TIME: 3–4 MINUTES

A stunningly attractive combination of colors, textures, and oriental flavors make this a sumptuous stir-fry. Long beans, or yard beans as they are called in Malaysia, are very crunchy when young and add a lovely bite to this dish.

1 **garlic** clove, crushed

½ pound **long** or **string beans**, cut into 1½-inch lengths

2 large **tomatoes**, cut into eighths, or 8 **cherry tomatoes**

4 **Chinese leaves**, cut into 2-inch diamond-shaped pieces

1 tablespoon **light soy sauce**

1 tablespoon **oyster sauce**

1 teaspoon **sugar**

freshly ground **black pepper**

3 tablespoons **sunflower oil**

1 **ASSEMBLE** all the ingredients.

2 **HEAT** a wok, add the oil, and, when hot, stir-fry the garlic without letting it brown.

3 **ADD** the beans immediately and toss well 30 seconds, then add the tomatoes and Chinese leaves, stirring all the time.

4 **ADD** the soy and oyster sauces, sugar, and pepper to taste. Cook 1 minute, then serve at once so that the vegetables remain crisp.

STUFFED OMELETS *KAI YAT SAI*

**SERVES 2–4   PREPARATION TIME: 12–15 MINUTES
COOKING TIME: 15 MINUTES**

Kai yat sai *is commonly served as a midday lunch dish and can be bought from stands and cafés. Rarely found on restaurant menus, these omelets are ideal for people in a hurry.*

---

3 **garlic** cloves, chopped

8 **black peppercorns**

6 **cilantro** stems

4 tablespoons **sunflower oil**

¼ pound ground **pork**

1 **onion**, chopped

¼ pound **sugar snap peas** or **snow peas**, sliced finely

1 **tomato**, seeded and chopped

1 teaspoon **sugar**

6 large **eggs**

1 tablespoon **fish sauce**

1 **POUND** the garlic, peppercorns, and cilantro roots and stalks (reserve the leaves for the garnish) to a juicy paste using a mortar and pestle.

2 **HEAT** half the oil in a warmed wok. Fry the paste, which will give off a rich aroma. Immediately add the pork and stir-fry until it changes color.

3 **ADD** the onion, sugar snap peas or snow peas, and tomato, stir-frying 1 minute between each addition, then stir in the sugar, and set the wok aside.

4 **BEAT** the eggs and fish sauce together in a bowl. Heat half the remaining oil in a large skillet over medium heat.

5 **POUR** in half the eggs and tilt the pan until the surface is evenly coated. Keep lifting the mixture from the edges of the pan so that the raw egg mixture moves there and becomes cooked. When the omelet is cooked on one side but still creamy on top, spoon half the pork mixture down the center of the omelet. Fold both sides over the filling, then slide the omelet on to a warm plate. Keep warm.

6 **REPEAT** the process with the remaining ingredients to make a second omelet. Cut both omelets in half and garnish with the cilantro leaves.

SWEET AND SOUR FISH *PLA PRIEW-WAAN*

**SERVES 2–4   PREPARATION TIME: 15 MINUTES
COOKING TIME: 15–20 MINUTES**

Whole red mullet, snapper, or sea bass crisp-fried then served smothered in a rich, red, sweet and sour sauce with the fragrance of ginger and the flavor of Chinese mushrooms, garnished with pineapple slices, shredded chilies, and cilantro leaves.

4 **Chinese mushrooms**

1 whole **red mullet**, **snapper**, or **sea bass**
    (1½ pounds), cleaned and scaled

1 tablespoon seasoned **flour**

1¼ cups **sunflower oil**

1 **garlic** clove, crushed

1 **onion**, finely sliced

½-inch piece fresh **ginger**, peeled and
    finely shredded

generous ¾ cup **water**

2 tablespoons **rice vinegar**

5 tablespoons **tomato ketchup**

2 tablespoons **fish sauce**

1 teaspoon **cornstarch**

1–2 **chilies**, seeded and sliced finely to garnish

1–2 slices **pineapple**, cut into wedges to garnish

cilantro leaves to garnish

1 SOAK the Chinese mushrooms in warm water 20–30 minutes, then drain. Meanwhile, rinse the fish and dry well with paper towels. Coat in the seasoned flour and, depending on the size of the skillet, either leave whole or remove the head to make it fit the pan, cook separately, then push together to serve. If you choose a very large fish, it can be cut in half, cooked, and reassembled for serving.

2 POUR the oil into a skillet so that it is about 1 inch deep and cook the fish 5–7 minutes on each side, or until cooked through. Drain on paper towels and keep warm.

3 SPOON the remainder of the oil from cooking the fish into a clean skillet. Fry the garlic, onion, and ginger to bring out the flavors.

4 BLEND the water, vinegar, tomato ketchup, and fish sauce together and pour into the pan. Discard the mushroom stems, slice the caps finely, and add to the pan, then cook 3–4 minutes.

5 BLEND the cornstarch to a paste with 1 tablespoon water, then stir into the sauce to thicken.

6 POUR the sauce over the fish and serve garnished with the chilies, pineapple, and cilantro.

FRIED WHOLE FISH WITH TAMARIND SAUCE

PLA JIEN

SERVES 2–4   PREPARATION TIME: 20 MINUTES
COOKING TIME: 20 MINUTES

The sharpness of tamarind juice offsets the sweetness of fried snapper, bream, or sea bass and is complemented by the flavors of ginger, chilies, and soy sauce.

---

1 whole **red snapper**, **sea bass**, or **bream**
(1½ pounds), cleaned and scaled

2 tablespoons seasoned **cornstarch**

1¼ cups **sunflower oil**

TAMARIND SAUCE:

1 ounce **tamarind pulp**

2–3 **garlic** cloves, chopped

4–6 **scallions**, white parts only, cut into
short lengths

½-inch piece fresh **ginger**, peeled and
finely shredded

1 tablespoon **soy sauce**

1–2 tablespoons **dark brown sugar**

1–2 tablespoons **fish sauce**

1–2 **red chilies**, seeded and shredded
to garnish

1 **SOAK** the tamarind pulp in a generous ½ cup warm water 10 minutes, then strain (see page 20).

2 **RINSE** the fish and dry well with paper towels. Coat in the seasoned cornstarch and, depending on the size of the skillet, either leave whole or remove the head to make it fit the pan, cook separately, then push together to serve. If you choose a very large fish, it can be cut in half, cooked, and reassembled for serving.

3 **POUR** the oil into a skillet so that it is about 1 inch deep, and cook the fish 5–7 minutes on each side, or until cooked through. Drain on paper towels and keep warm.

4 **FRY** the garlic in 2 tablespoons of the oil from cooking the fish. Add the scallions and ginger. Keep moving the ingredients around so that they do not brown.

5 **ADD** the soy sauce, sugar, fish sauce, and tamarind juice, tasting until you have the right balance of sweet, sour, and salty flavors.

6 **POUR** this sauce over the fish and serve garnished with the chilies.

FRIED BEAN CURD WITH PEANUT SAUCE AND CUCUMBER SALAD *TAO-HOO TAWD*

SERVES 4   PREPARATION TIME: 20 MINUTES   COOKING TIME: 10 MINUTES

Slices of soft, fresh bean curd, carefully fried in garlic-flavored oil then bathed in a rich spicy peanut sauce, garnished with crushed peanuts and cilantro leaves, and served with a deceptively spicy cucumber salad and crispy shrimp chips.

4 tablespoons **sunflower oil**

1 **garlic** clove, crushed

¼ pound **fresh bean curd**, drained, cut in half, and sliced

1 recipe quantity **peanut sauce** *(see page 28)*

cilantro leaves to garnish

shrimp chips *(see page 53)* to serve

CUCUMBER SALAD:

½ **cucumber**, halved, seeded, and thinly sliced

6 **shallots** or 1 small **red onion**, finely sliced

3–4 tablespoons **basic dipping sauce** or **sweet chili dipping sauce** *(see page 27)*

1 **red chili**, seeded and finely sliced to garnish

scant ¼ cup **peanuts**, crushed to garnish

sweet basil or **cilantro leaves** to garnish

1 PREPARE the cucumber salad. Salt the cucumber, then rinse, and drain. Place in a serving dish with the shallots or onion and spoon over the dipping sauce. Cover with plastic wrap and chill until required.

2 HEAT the oil in a wok and fry the garlic over gentle heat, then fry the bean curd slices on both sides with care so that they do not break up. Drain well on crumpled paper towels.

3 ARRANGE the bean curd on a serving dish and pour over the hot peanut sauce. Garnish with cilantro leaves.

4 TOP the cucumber salad with the sliced chili, peanuts, and basil or cilantro leaves. Serve the bean curd with the salad and shrimp chips.

DEEP-FRIED NOODLES WITH SWEET AND SAVORY SAUCE *MEE KROB*

SERVES **4**   PREPARATION TIME: **15** MINUTES   COOKING TIME: **20** MINUTES

2 **eggs**, beaten with 2 tablespoons **water**

salt and freshly ground **black pepper**

6 tablespoons **sunflower oil**, plus extra for deep-frying

4 **shallots** or 1 **red onion**, sliced to garnish

2 ounces **dried shrimp** to garnish

⅓ pound **fresh bean curd**, cut into small cubes

1 cooked **chicken breast**, cut into thin strips

2 tablespoons **tomato paste**

½ cup **water**

1 tablespoon **rice vinegar**

1 teaspoon **salt**

¼ cup **sugar**

6 ounces **rice vermicelli noodles**

generous 1 cup **bean sprouts** to garnish

2 **scallions**, shredded to garnish

2 **red chilies**, seeded and sliced to garnish

cilantro leaves to garnish

1 **SEASON** the beaten egg. Heat a wok or skillet and add 2 tablespoons of the oil. Pour in the beaten egg and make an omelet. Place on a plate, roll into a sausage shape, and allow to cool, then cut into neat pieces. Set aside for a garnish.

2 **ADD** the remaining 4 tablespoons of the oil to the wok and fry the shallots or onion until golden, then drain on paper towels. Add the dried shrimp to the same oil and fry until crisp, then drain.

3 **POUR** the oil into a bowl, discard the sediment, then return the oil to the wok. Fry the bean curd until just coloring, then drain on paper towels. Add the chicken, tomato paste, water, vinegar, salt, and sugar to the pan and cook to a glossy tomato sauce. Pour into a bowl and set aside. Clean the wok ready for the noodles.

4 **HEAT** the oil for deep-frying in the wok to 375°F no more than 30 minutes before serving. Crush the noodles lightly in a plastic bag.

5 **FRY** handfuls of the noodles very briefly—they will puff up and become crisp almost as soon as they are dropped into the hot oil. Remove at once before they take on any color. Drain on paper towels.

6 **PLACE** the noodles in a large bowl and add the warmed sauce. Mix well, finally adding the fried bean curd. Place on a serving dish.

7 **GARNISH** the edge with the bean sprouts, omelet, and scallions. Scatter the top with onion, dried shrimp, chili, and cilantro.

SPICED EGGPLANT WITH YELLOW BEAN SAUCE *MAKUA PAT PRIK*

SERVES 4   PREPARATION TIME: 12–15 MINUTES
COOKING TIME: 7–8 MINUTES

*Almost a meal in itself, this rich assembly of jewel-like vegetables
is a winner whether served hot, warm, or cold.*

---

3 tablespoons **sunflower oil**

1–2 **garlic** cloves, crushed

2 **red** or **green chilies**, seeded and finely sliced

½ pound **purple eggplant**, cut into quarters
  lengthwise, then sliced at an angle

4 tablespoons **chicken** or **vegetable stock**
  (*see page 23*)

1 **pepper**, seeded and cut into diamonds

2 tablespoons **crushed yellow bean sauce**

1 tablespoon **light soy sauce**

1 teaspoon **sugar**

1 **sweet basil** sprig, leaves only to garnish

1 **HEAT** a wok, add the oil, and, when hot, fry the garlic and most of the
chilies over gentle heat until just softening.

2 **ADD** the eggplant pieces and keep turning, then pour in the stock.
Turn all the time until the eggplant pieces are softening, then add
the peppers.

3 **BLEND** together the crushed yellow bean sauce, soy sauce, and sugar.
Add to the wok. Stir gently, then cover, and cook a further 3 minutes
over gentle heat. Taste for seasoning.

4 **PLACE** in a warm serving bowl, garnish with the reserved chilies and
lots of basil leaves. Serve hot.

STEAMED MUSSELS WITH LEMONGRASS AND BASIL *HOY MALANGPOO NEUNG*

**SERVES 4   PREPARATION TIME: 25–30 MINUTES
COOKING TIME: 5–6 MINUTES**

The most fragrant mussels you will ever eat—steamed in a wok with lemongrass, sweet basil, and lime leaves and served with a stunning chili fish sauce.

2¼ pounds **mussels**

4 **lemongrass** stems, bruised

3 **lime leaves**, torn

4 **sweet basil** sprigs, leaves only

1¼ cups boiling **water**

CHILI FISH SAUCE:

juice of 1 large **lemon**

2 **garlic** cloves, crushed

4–6 **bird's eye chilies**, seeded if wished, then chopped or pounded

3 tablespoons **fish sauce**

2 teaspoons **sugar**

1 SCRUB each mussel carefully and remove any beards. Discard any with broken shells or those that are already open. Keep in a large container covered with water in the refrigerator until required.

2 BLEND all the sauce ingredients together in a bowl and set aside.

3 LINE the base of a wok or a steamer that is large enough to cook all the mussels with bruised lemongrass stems, torn lime leaves, and most of the basil leaves.

4 HEAT the wok, add the mussels, and keep over high heat. Pour in the boiling water. Cover closely and steam about 5 minutes, or until the shells are open. Discard any that do not open in this time.

5 SPOON the mussels on to serving plates. Discard the flavoring herbs using a slotted spoon so that the juices remain in the wok.

6 REHEAT the juices until hot and add the prepared chili fish sauce. Cook briefly, then spoon over the mussels on the serving plates, and scatter over the remaining basil leaves to garnish.

STEAMED WHOLE FISH WITH PRESERVED PLUMS IN BANANA LEAF PARCEL *PLA NEUNG BOUY*

**SERVES 2–4   PREPARATION TIME: 10 MINUTES
COOKING TIME: 10–15 MINUTES**

Carp or sea bream flavored with a heady mixture of chopped preserved plums, fresh ginger, peppers, onions, and typical Thai sauces, steamed almost to melting moistness and served garnished with scallions and fragrant cilantro.

1 whole **carp** or **sea bream** (1 pound), cleaned, or fillets if preferred

1 **banana leaf**

3 **preserved plums**, chopped

½-inch piece fresh **ginger**, grated or cut into matchsticks

¼ **onion**, thinly sliced

¼ each **green** and **red pepper**, seeded and sliced

2 tablespoons **light soy sauce**

1 tablespoon **oyster sauce**

½ teaspoon **sugar**

2 tablespoons **sunflower oil**

2 **scallions**, white parts left whole and tops shredded

1 small handful **cilantro leaves** to garnish

1 RINSE and dry the fish. Slash whole fish three times on each side.

2 PLUNGE the banana leaf into boiling water to clean it and make it pliable. Cut it into two 12-inch squares and stack these on a lightly oiled plate that will fit into a steaming basket or on a trivet, whichever you are using. Place the fish on the squares.

3 SCATTER the chopped plums over the fish with the ginger, onion, and peppers. Mix together the soy and oyster sauces, sugar, and oil, then spoon over the fish. Top with the white parts of the scallions. Fold into a loose package and secure with toothpicks or satay sticks.

4 LIFT the plate into a wok or steamer over boiling water and cover closely with a lid. Steam 8–10 minutes for fillets or 15 minutes for a whole fish, or until the fish is tender. Test with a skewer in the thickest part.

5 LIFT out of the steamer and serve on the cooking plate, garnished with the shredded scallion tops and the cilantro leaves.

STEAMED STUFFED CRABS *POO-JAR*

**SERVES 4   PREPARATION TIME: 20 MINUTES
COOKING TIME: 10–15 MINUTES**

Crab meat blended with finely ground lean pork, fresh cilantro, ginger, and garlic, packed into crab shells, then steamed before being served on a bed of lettuce with a piquant sauce. The recipe tells you how to dress crabs yourself if you need to.

4 small cooked **crabs** (about ½ pound each), ready-dressed if available

⅓ pound finely ground **pork**

3 **cilantro** stems

½-inch piece fresh **ginger**, finely chopped

2 **garlic** cloves, crushed

1–2 tablespoons **fish sauce**

freshly ground **black pepper**

1 **egg**, separated

lettuce leaves to serve

SAUCE:

2–3 **red** or **green chilies**, seeded and sliced

juice of 1 **lemon**

1 tablespoon **sugar**

6 tablespoons **fish sauce**

1 REMOVE the crab claws, place each crab on its back with the head away from you. Use your thumbs to push the body from the main shell. Discard the stomach sac and lungs (sometimes called "dead men's fingers") and any green matter.

2 SCOOP out all the edible meat into a bowl and add the meat from the cracked claws. (If the crabs are ready-dressed, all this will have been done for you; simply scoop the meat into a bowl.)

3 ADD the pork, cilantro stalks, and some of the leaves with the ginger, garlic, fish sauce, and pepper, then mix well.

4 BEAT the egg white lightly and use this to bind the pork mixture, then spoon the stuffing neatly into the crab shells. Brush the egg yolk over the stuffing to seal.

5 PREPARE the sauce by pounding the chilies with the lemon juice, sugar, and fish sauce to taste using a mortar and pestle. Pour into a bowl.

6 PLACE the crabs in a steamer basket or on a trivet over boiling water, cover, and steam 10–15 minutes.

7 SERVE with some lettuce leaves on a dish and garnish with the remaining cilantro leaves. Pass around the sauce to drizzle on top of each crab as it is eaten.

GRILLED WHOLE FISH WITH HOT AND SOUR CHILI SAUCE *PLA POW*

SERVES **4**　PREPARATION TIME: **10** MINUTES, PLUS **30** MINUTES MARINATING TIME　COOKING TIME: **8–10** MINUTES

Whole pomfret or mackerel, smothered in a garlic, cilantro, and oyster sauce, then grilled to a deep caramel color and served with chili sauce. Use whole fish for this; it looks so much more attractive—an important aspect of Thai cuisine.

2 **pomfret** or **mackerel** (¾ pound each), cleaned

4 **cilantro** stems

2 **garlic** cloves

1 teaspoon freshly ground **black pepper**

4 tablespoons **oyster sauce**

lime wedges to serve

HOT AND SOUR CHILI SAUCE:

5 tablespoons **fish sauce**

juice of 2 **limes** or **lemons**

2–3 **bird's eye chilies**, seeded, if liked, and finely sliced

2 tablespoons **palm** or **light brown sugar**

1 small handful **mint leaves**

1 RINSE and dry the fish and slash the skin three times on each side so that the flavors will permeate the flesh.

2 POUND the cilantro stalks with the garlic using a mortar and pestle (reserving the leaves for garnish). Add the black pepper and oyster sauce.

3 SMOTHER the fish on both sides with this mixture and set aside to marinate at least 30 minutes.

4 PREPARE the hot and sour chili sauce by placing all the ingredients in a bowl and blending them together.

5 HEAT the broiler to high and place the fish on a lightly oiled trivet in a broiler pan. Turn the broiler down to medium and place the fish under it. Cook about 4–5 minutes on each side, turning once during cooking, making sure the fish doesn't brown too quickly. (Strips of foil placed under the fish may aid in turning it.)

6 SERVE on a hot serving dish, garnished with the mint and reserved cilantro leaves and the prepared sauce. Provide lime wedges to squeeze over the fish, which will often be filleted at the table when you order this dish in a Thai restaurant.

BEEF WITH COCONUT

PRA RAAM LONG SONG

**SERVES 4   PREPARATION TIME: 25 MINUTES
COOKING TIME: 1¼–1¾ HOURS**

King Rama had a pool in which he loved to swim. This beef in a creamy sauce surrounded by freshly cooked greens is supposed to represent his bathing paradise!

3⅓ cups canned **coconut milk**

generous ¾ cup **water**

1 tablespoon **soy sauce**

¾ cup **peanuts**, half lightly crushed

2¼ pounds good-quality **chuck steak**, sliced across the grain into even-size pieces

6 **shallots** or 1 **onion**, sliced

6 **garlic** cloves, sliced

1-inch piece fresh **ginger**, cut into matchsticks

1 **lemongrass** stem, lower 2½ inches sliced

1 teaspoon **chili powder**

1 tablespoon **dark brown sugar**

1–2 tablespoons **fish sauce**

1 pound **spinach**, **curly kale**, or **mustard greens**

1 **red chili**, shredded to garnish

1 **RESERVE** one-quarter of the coconut milk and place the remainder plus the water in a large saucepan with the soy sauce and whole peanuts.

2 **ADD** the meat and slowly bring to a boil, then turn the heat down, cover the pan, and simmer gently 1–1½ hours until the meat is tender.

3 **PLACE** the shallots or onion, garlic, ginger, and slices of lemongrass in a food processor with the chili powder and blend to a paste.

4 **TEST** the beef with a skewer. About 20 minutes before the cooking time is up, spoon half the reserved coconut milk into a wok and heat gently until bubbling. Add the spice paste to this, stirring all the time, to bring out the full flavors.

5 **ADD** this mixture to the beef in the pan and continue to cook a further 15 minutes. Add the sugar and fish sauce to taste.

6 **PLUNGE** the spinach leaves, kale, or mustard greens into a saucepan of boiling water, then drain thoroughly, and arrange on the serving dish. Spoon the meat and sauce on to the greens and scatter with the lightly crushed peanuts. Top with the remaining coconut milk and garnish with shredded chili.

THAI-STYLE CASSEROLE OF DUCK *PED TUN*

SERVES 4   PREPARATION TIME: 20 MINUTES, PLUS 1½ HOURS
MARINATING TIME   COOKING TIME: 1¼–1¾ HOURS

---

5 pound **duck**, divided into quarters, or 4 **duck** portions

4 **cilantro** stems

8 **garlic** cloves

1 teaspoon **black peppercorns**

1 tablespoon **brandy** or **whiskey**

6–8 **Chinese mushrooms**

1 teaspoon each **coriander** and **cumin seeds**

3 tablespoons **sunflower oil**

2¼ cups **duck** or **chicken stock** (see page 23)

2 tablespoons **light soy sauce**

1 tablespoon **dark soy sauce**

salt

3 tablespoons **cornstarch**, blended to a paste with 6 tablespoons **water**

1 WASH and dry the duck, then cut into two breast and two leg portions, if whole. Use the carcass to make stock.

2 CRUSH the cilantro stalks (reserving the leaves for garnish) with the garlic and peppercorns using a mortar and pestle and add the brandy or whiskey.

3 RUB this mixture into the duck portions and set aside to marinate 1½ hours. Meanwhile, soak the Chinese mushrooms in 1¼ cups water 20–30 minutes, then drain, reserving the soaking liquid. Discard the mushroom stems and slice the caps.

4 DRY-FRY the coriander and cumin seeds in a hot wok a few minutes, then pound them using a mortar and pestle.

5 HEAT the oil in the same wok and add the duck portions. Fry until brown and sealed on all sides then transfer to a casserole, add the stock and reserved soaking liquid, the mushrooms, coriander and cumin seeds, soy sauces, and a little salt to taste.

6 COVER and simmer gently 1–1½ hours until tender.

7 LET cool, then skim off any fat from the sauce. Lift the duck from the stock and discard the skin. Divide each portion in half.

8 REHEAT the liquid and add the blended cornstarch to thicken the sauce, stirring until it comes to a boil. Add the duck and reheat gently. Garnish with the cilantro leaves.

KING SHRIMP, NOODLES, AND MUSHROOMS IN A CLAY POT *GOONG OB MOR-DIN*

SERVES 4   PREPARATION TIME: 20–25 MINUTES
COOKING TIME: 25 MINUTES

King shrimp, marinated in a peppery sauce, layered with bean thread noodles and straw mushrooms, then baked and served with a fiery chili and ginger sauce.

4 ounces **bean thread noodles**

16–18 raw **jumbo shrimp** (about 1 pound), shelled, heads removed but tails on

2 **garlic** cloves, crushed

2 **cilantro** stems

6 **black peppercorns** and 6–8 fresh **green peppercorns**, if available

2 tablespoons **light** or **mushroom soy sauce**

3 tablespoons **fish sauce**

3 tablespoons **sunflower oil**

6 **Chinese leaves**, 4 left whole and 2 sliced

1 can **straw mushrooms** (7 ounces) or ¼ pound **button mushrooms**, sliced

1 recipe quantity **sweet chili dipping sauce** (*see page 27*)

1-inch piece fresh **ginger**, unpeeled and cut into fine matchsticks

1 **HEAT** the oven to 425°F.

2 **SOAK** the bean thread noodles in warm water 10 minutes, then drain, and cut into short lengths with scissors.

3 **SLIT** the shrimp along the back and remove the black vein, then put them into a bowl.

4 **POUND** the garlic with the cilantro stalks (reserving the leaves for garnish), both peppercorns, if using, soy or mushroom sauce, and 2 tablespoons of the fish sauce. Pour over the shrimp and mix well.

5 **BRUSH** the inside of a clay pot or a 5 cup casserole with some of the oil, then line with the four whole Chinese leaves. (This protects the shrimp and keeps the dish moist.)

6 **ARRANGE** the snipped noodles, sliced mushrooms, and marinated shrimp on top and drizzle with the remaining oil. Top with the sliced Chinese leaves, cover with a lid, and bake in the heated oven 25 minutes.

7 **MIX** the dipping sauce with the remaining fish sauce and the ginger.

8 **SERVE** the dish at once garnished with the reserved cilantro leaves. Drizzle the chili sauce on top of each helping.

BARBECUE SPARERIBS

KHRONG MOO YANG

SERVES 4   PREPARATION TIME: 10–12 MINUTES, PLUS 1 HOUR
MARINATING TIME   COOKING TIME: 40–45 MINUTES

*The honey in the marinade tenderizes the ribs, making the flesh meltingly tender.
The dark brown, glossy sauce, flecked with sesame seeds, tastes as good as it looks.*

2¼ pounds meaty **pork spareribs**,
    cut into 4 inch lengths by the butcher

1 teaspoon **sesame seeds**

MARINADE:

3 **cilantro** stems

¾ cup **honey** or **light corn syrup**, warmed

1 tablespoon **dark brown sugar**

2 tablespoons **fish sauce**

1 tablespoon **soy sauce**

1 teaspoon **five spice powder**

1 **garlic** clove, crushed

1 **ARRANGE** the ribs in a noncorrosive shallow container.

2 **POUND** the cilantro stalks finely using a mortar and pestle (reserving the leaves for the garnish) and put into a bowl with the remaining marinade ingredients. Mix well, then pour over the ribs and let marinate 1 hour, turning twice.

3 **HEAT** the oven to 400°F.

4 **ARRANGE** the ribs on a trivet in a roasting pan. Sprinkle with the sesame seeds. Cover the base of the roasting pan with ¾ inch water.

5 **COOK** uncovered in the heated oven 40–45 minutes. Use the remaining marinade to baste twice during cooking to keep the ribs moist and enhance the flavor. The honey in the marinade will give the ribs a lacquered look, so turn the ribs if you feel that they are taking on too much color before the meat is cooked through, and turn down the oven temperature.

6 **SERVE** the ribs on a plate garnished with the cilantro leaves.

BARBECUE CHICKEN *GAI YANG*

SERVES 4   PREPARATION TIME: 5 MINUTES, PLUS 1–2 HOURS MARINATING TIME   COOKING TIME: 35–40 MINUTES

Chicken breasts or legs are slashed a couple of times through the fleshy part to allow the Thai marinade to permeate the meat before being roasted or barbecued to golden succulence. This is a recipe you will make over and over again.

4 **chicken** portions

1 recipe quantity **cucumber salad**
  (*see page 146*)

MARINADE:

4 **cilantro** stems

1 tablespoon **coriander seeds**

2 tablespoons **light corn syrup** or **honey**

1 teaspoon **black peppercorns**,
  coarsely ground

2–3 **garlic** cloves, crushed

2 tablespoons **fish** or **light soy sauce**

2 teaspoons **ground turmeric**

1 SLASH the chicken pieces and place in a noncorrosive container.

2 POUND the cilantro stalks finely using a mortar and pestle (reserving the leaves for the garnish) and dry-fry the coriander seeds in a skillet 2 minutes before crushing.

3 PLACE in a bowl with the remaining marinade ingredients. Mix well, then pour over the chicken pieces, and let marinate 1–2 hours, turning several times.

4 HEAT the oven to 375°F.

5 ROAST the chicken pieces in the heated oven 35–40 minutes in a roasting pan, or barbecue or broil, turning frequently until tender and golden. (Alternatively, you could part-cook the meat in the oven 25–30 minutes, then transfer to the barbecue for excellent results.)

6 SERVE the chicken garnished with the reserved cilantro leaves and accompanied by the cucumber salad.

COCONUT MILK ICE CREAM

ALSA KHRIM KA-THI

**SERVES 6　PREPARATION TIME: 12–15 MINUTES, PLUS 45 MINUTES
FREEZING TIME　COOKING TIME: 4–5 MINUTES**

This sumptuous, creamy ice cream could not be easier to make, and contains very few ingredients. The taste of coconut, which is inevitably linked with Thai meals, takes center stage here, making a suitable end to an oriental meal.

1 cup **superfine sugar**

½ cup **water**

3⅓ cups canned **coconut milk**

6 teaspoons toasted **dried coconut (unsweetened)** to decorate

1 **HEAT** the sugar and water in a saucepan and stir over gentle heat until the sugar dissolves. Continue cooking until the sugar starts to thicken, then remove from the heat, and let cool 20 minutes.

2 **ADD** the coconut milk and stir to mix well.

3 **POUR** into an ice cream machine and churn about 45 minutes, or until you achieve the right consistency. Store in the freezer until needed.

4 **TAKE** it out of the freezer as your guests arrive and let it soften slightly in the refrigerator. (Coconut milk ice cream must be kept cold because it melts rapidly.)

5 **SPOON** into bowls and top with a little freshly toasted coconut.

FRIED BANANAS

KLUAY TORD

SERVES 4   PREPARATION TIME: 8 MINUTES   COOKING TIME: 5 MINUTES

Bananas are often underrated as a dessert, but not by the Thais. This dessert is best made while your guests wait at the table, since you can prepare it in no time at all. Try these toffeeish bananas with sweet glutinous rice (see page 174).

4 fresh **bananas**

½ stick **butter**

4 heaped tablespoons **palm** or **brown sugar**

juice of 2 **limes**

4 tablespoons **coconut milk**

1 PEEL the bananas and either slice each one diagonally into four thick slices or slice lengthwise then halve again for a softer result (as prepared in the weekend lunch with friends' menu, page 200).

2 MELT the butter in a skillet or wok and add the banana slices. Fry them on both sides over medium heat until golden and soft.

3 SPRINKLE in the sugar and stir over the heat until it dissolves and thickens to a syrup.

4 TRANSFER the bananas and sauce to sundae dishes if cut into slices or on to plates if cut more thinly. Squeeze over the lime juice and drizzle the coconut milk on top, and serve.

GLUTINOUS RICE WITH MANGO SLICES

KHAO NIEW MAMOUNG

SERVES 6   PREPARATION TIME: 20 MINUTES, PLUS 1–2 HOURS RESTING TIME

This may not be a show-stopper to look at, but that is more than made up for by the glorious balance of coconut-flavored sticky rice with the golden sun-drenched mangoes cut into arc-shaped slices, topped with shreds of lime zest.

1¼ cups canned **coconut milk**

¼ cup **superfine sugar**

good pinch of **salt**

1 recipe quantity **glutinous rice** (*see page 29*)

2 ripe **mangoes**

lime zest, shredded thinly to decorate

1 **STIR** the coconut milk, sugar, and salt together in a bowl until the sugar has dissolved. Pour into a serving bowl, then tip in the cooked glutinous rice. Mix well. Cover and leave on one side 1–2 hours until the rice has absorbed the coconut milk.

2 **PEEL** the mangoes with a vegetable peeler. Slide a sharp knife as near to the pit as possible while holding the mango on a cutting board in a horizontal position. Cut on either side of the pit, then slice the mango into long, neat slices. Transfer to a covered container and leave in the refrigerator until required.

3 **SPOON** the rice into individual serving bowls, top with slices of mango, and decorate with shreds of lime zest.

EXOTIC FRUITS WITH JASMINE-FLAVORED SYRUP *RUAM MIT*

SERVES 4   PREPARATION TIME: 20 MINUTES   COOKING TIME: 5 MINUTES

Tangy oranges, sweet fragrant mango, and lychees in a rich syrup, delicately flavored with jasmine essence, then topped with crushed ice—an unforgettable experience. The jasmine flavor adds an especially exotic touch.

generous 1 cup **water**

½ cup **sugar**

few drops **jasmine water**, to taste
(if unavailable, use either **rose water**
or **orange flower water**)

4 **oranges**, segmented

8 **lychees** or **rambutans**, peeled but left
whole, or can of either (1¼ pounds), drained

1 **mango**, peeled and sliced either side of the pit
(*see page 178*), **then cut into cubes**

crushed **ice**

orchid flowers (optional)

1 **PLACE** the water and sugar in a heavy-based saucepan over low heat. Stir until the sugar has dissolved, then increase the heat, and boil 5 minutes. Cool to room temperature, then add the flavoring water and chill.

2 **PLACE** the prepared fruits in a serving bowl. Cover and chill.

3 **POUR** the chilled and flavored syrup over the fruits just before serving. Top with a little crushed ice and decorate with orchid flowers, if you wish.

PINEAPPLE BUTTERFLIES *SUB PA ROS*

SERVES 4   PREPARATION TIME: 10–15 MINUTES

This is a very attractive yet simple way to serve pineapple. Cover and chill before serving, possibly with the fresh mango (see below). Buy both pineapples and mangoes a few days before you need them to give them time to mature.

1 ripe **pineapple** with yellow flesh

banana leaves

1 WASH and dry the pineapple, cut off the top and bottom and discard, then cut it in half from top to bottom. Place each half cut-side up.

2 CUT a V-shaped groove down the center of the core of one of the halves.

3 FORM the antennae and the top of the wings of the butterfly by making a cut angled toward the center from both borders of the core. Now make a shallow curving slice from the peel on both sides and remove the flesh from the peel in one piece.

4 TURN the pineapple half curved side up. Cut a single groove down the most rounded part of the curve to mark the end of the body and two parallel grooves at equal distances down the sides to separate the wings.

5 REPEAT on the other half then cut the pineapple into ½-inch slices.

6 ARRANGE the pineapple butterflies on a banana leaf-lined plate.

VARIATION   FRESH MANGO   *MAMUANG SUK*

Wash two ripe mangoes. Place them on a chopping board and, using a sharp, broad-bladed knife and starting from the stem end, with the blade parallel to the fruit and the board, cut as close to the central pit as possible. Turn the fruit over and repeat. Now you have two perfect halves. Cut in one direction several times close together, then in the same way in the opposite direction to make a criss-cross pattern, taking care not to cut all the way through the skin. With your fingers underneath the fruit, push up and the fruit pieces will rise in a pattern like a hedgehog's prickles.

ORIENTAL FRUIT PLATTER

POLAMAI RUAM

Here are some of the fruits that might be included in a fruit platter. They will inevitably vary with the seasons, but there will always be enough fabulous fruits to make a spectacular dish. Line the serving plate with a banana leaf cut to fit.

1 banana leaf

2 mangosteens

4 lychees

4 rambutans

1 star fruit

1 PLUNGE the banana leaf into boiling water to make it supple, then cut a piece to fit the serving plate and put it in its place.

2 CUT the shell of the mangosteens all the way around the middle with a sharp knife, being careful not to cut into the flesh of the fruit (the shell is usually about ¼ inch thick). Lift off the top of the shell to reveal the creamy white segments nestling in the lower half. Place the opened fruits on the banana leaf.

3 PLACE the lychees on the plate as they are. (To eat, simply crack them open with your fingers and pull them apart to reveal the opalescent fruit around a large brown pit.)

4 CUT the rambutans around the middle, remove the top, and display the fruit rather like a boiled egg in a hairy cup. (To eat, hold the bottom part in your fingers and pull out the fruit with your teeth. There is a brown pit in the center.)

5 CUT the star fruit, or carambola, into horizontal slices to preserve its star shape, and add to the plate.

PUMPKIN FILLED
WITH COCONUT CUSTARD *SANGKAYA PHAK THONG*

SERVES **4—6**   PREPARATION TIME: **20** MINUTES, PLUS OVERNIGHT
CHILLING TIME   COOKING TIME: **30** MINUTES

The bright orange pumpkin flesh contrasts with the creamy coconut custard filling to create a spectacular dessert. This is a popular sweet throughout Thailand.

1 small, firm whole **pumpkin**, about 8 inches in diameter (2 pounds in weight); choose a size that will fit in your steamer

4 **eggs**

⅔ cup **coconut milk**, slightly warmed

2 tablespoons **palm** or **white sugar**

1 **CUT** the top from the pumpkin carefully and remove the cap to expose the seeded center. Spoon out the seeds and some of the flesh to insure the custard mixture will just fill the cavity. Be careful you do not cut through the flesh at the base. If it is tough, presteam the pumpkin 10 minutes upside down. Drain well.

2 **PLACE** the pumpkin on two strips of foil to make it easier to lift in and out of the steamer.

3 **BEAT** the eggs with the slightly warmed coconut milk and sugar until well blended. Strain into a large measuring cup.

4 **POUR** the coconut mixture into the pumpkin, but do not replace the cap. Place the pumpkin in the steamer over boiling water 20–30 minutes, or until the custard is set and the pumpkin flesh is cooked. Test with a skewer: It should come out clean.

5 **REMOVE** the pan from the heat and allow to cool before lifting the pumpkin out of the pan using the foil straps.

6 **COVER** and chill overnight. Cut into wedges to serve with a selection of fresh fruit slices or a sherbet.

MANGO SHERBET *MAMUANG*

SERVES 6   PREPARATION TIME: 15 MINUTES, PLUS 1¼ HOURS COOLING TIME AND UP TO 7 HOURS FREEZING TIME   COOKING TIME: 8 MINUTES

Eating a golden mango is like tasting liquid sunshine, and this simple method of serving the fruit makes the most of its golden color and fragrant taste.

---

2 large **mangoes** (about 1 pound each), peeled

½ cup **water**

⅔ cup **sugar**

2-inch piece fresh **ginger**, peeled, half bruised and the other half cut into fine matchsticks

2 **limes**, zest shredded and juice squeezed

1 large **egg white**, lightly whisked

1 **PLACE** the mangoes on a chopping board and slice from stem end to tip with the flat of a knife, as close to the pit as possible on both sides. Place the flesh in a food processor and blend to a smooth puree.

2 **PLACE** the water and sugar in a saucepan with the bruised piece of ginger and heat to release the flavor, stirring until the sugar dissolves. Simmer 3–4 minutes, then remove from the heat, and let cool 10 minutes. Lift out the ginger and add the lime juice and matchsticks of ginger to the syrup. Cool at least 1 hour.

3 **POUR** boiling water over the lime zest in a saucepan and bring to a boil. Strain and let cool, reserving the lime shreds. Blend the mango puree and syrup together. Continue, following step 4 if you have an ice cream maker or step 5 if you do not.

4 **POUR** the mixture into an ice cream maker and churn until the mixture begins to thicken. Add the egg white and churn 10 minutes more then put into a container and keep in the freezer until required.

5 **POUR** the mixture into a container and place in the freezer about 2 hours. Remove and use a heavy whisk or large fork to break down the crystals. Refreeze and repeat after 1 hour and again after 2 hours. Add the egg white then freeze another 2 hours before serving.

6 **SERVE** decorated with the lime shreds.

THAI RUBIES IN SWEETENED COCONUT MILK *TUP TIM KROB*

SERVES 4   PREPARATION TIME: 15 MINUTES, PLUS 30 MINUTES SOAKING TIME   COOKING TIME: 8 MINUTES

Red rubies, green emeralds, or blue sapphires: The choice is yours for this popular desert. Just use the appropriate food coloring for the tiny cubes of water chestnut.

¾ cup **sugar**

1⅓ cups **water**

½ teaspoon **red food coloring**

1 can **water chestnuts** (8 ounces), drained

¼ cup **tapioca flour**

1⅔ cups canned **coconut milk**

1 **PLACE** the sugar and a generous ¾ cup of the water in a saucepan and stir over high heat until the sugar dissolves, then reduce the heat, and simmer 3 minutes. Set aside to cool.

2 **ADD** the food coloring to the remaining water.

3 **DICE** the water chestnuts by cutting them in three each way to make even-size pieces. Place in the colored water. Leave 30 minutes to take on a good color, then drain thoroughly in a metal strainer.

4 **SPOON** the tapioca flour into a plastic bag. Add the water chestnuts and toss until the dice are evenly coated. Place in a strainer and tap to remove the excess flour.

5 **BRING** a large pan of water to a full rolling boil. Tip in the colored water chestnuts. Stir lightly to prevent the "rubies" sinking. After 1–2 minutes the "rubies" will come to the surface. Carefully drain in a colander, then put immediately into a bowl of ice water to cool.

6 **MIX** the coconut milk and the cooled sugar syrup together in a measuring cup, then pour into serving bowls when ready to serve. Spoon in the "rubies" at the last minute and serve.

PART 3

THE MENUS

With so many **wonderful** dishes to choose from, cooking a Thai meal might seem a bit daunting. Which **dishes** go with which? How many dishes should be served? To help you plan and cook a Thai **meal**, I have put together a number of suggestions. Each has a time plan to assist in **organizing** your time and some hints on what you can do **beforehand** to prepare ingredients, so that some dishes can be prepared in advance and only need **finishing off** just before the meal is served. Handy preparation notes offer **hints** on certain aspects of preparation.

Once you have chosen a menu, plan the **shopping** and check the preparation notes. Read the recipes through and note the **preparations** that can be made ahead. Before you start cooking, make sure you have all the **equipment** you need, such as a wok or steamer, to hand, and that all your **ingredients** are assembled, particularly if you are going to cook a **stir-fry**.

Set the **table** with forks and spoons. (Never knives, since they are considered weapons.) Line dishes with banana leaves and place **orchids** in a bowl. (Such attention to detail is a hallmark of Thai **cuisine**.) Then just enjoy the experience of cooking and sharing the food with your **guests**.

SIMPLE LUNCH

TIME PLAN

Spicy corn cakes with a hint of lime leaves look very pretty on a lettuce-lined serving dish. The Chiang Mai curried noodle soup is a Northern Thai traditional dish. It is a spicy golden curry served with colorful accompaniments. Follow this with fresh fruit.

CORN CAKES
(see page 57)

CHIANG MAI CURRIED NOODLE SOUP WITH CHICKEN
(see page 70)

ORIENTAL FRUIT PLATTER
(see page 181)

The day before, buy the chicken, skin and joint it, and store in the refrigerator. Make the corn cake mixture and store in a covered container to form into corn cakes on the following day if time will be short. Halve all the recipe ingredients to prepare this meal for two.

AM
10:45 ASSEMBLE and prepare the ingredients for the soup; cut the chicken breasts into bite-size pieces and refrigerate in covered containers. Prepare the fruit platter.

11:15 ASSEMBLE and prepare all the garnishes for the soup. Fry the noodles. Place in small bowls and cover with plastic wrap.

11:45 FORM the corn cake mixture into small cakes. Place on a well-floured baking sheet to prevent sticking.

PM
12:00 MAKE the sweet chili dipping sauce or Thai relish.

12:15 COOK the soup to the end of step 3.

12:40 FRY the corn cakes, drain on paper towels, and keep warm in the oven.

1:15 SERVE the corn cakes with the dipping sauce or relish.

1:30 FINISH the soup and serve with the garnishes.

2:00 SERVE the fruit platter.

PREPARATION NOTES

BUY a whole chicken for a dish, instead of chicken portions. This is not only better value but also provides you with food for other meals. **CUT** each breast portion off the breastbone, and sever both legs where they are joined to the carcass, giving you four generous portions. **FREEZE** any pieces you aren't using that day, and use the carcass to make stock.

LUNCHBOX

Tired of sandwiches in the office? Then take a little time to prepare the tastiest lunchbox ever. The salad, full of tender beef strips and crunchy vegetables, is partnered by steamed fragrant rice and some delicious coconut crisps —perfect for nibbling on. Fresh fruit completes the meal.

COCONUT CRISPS

(see page 61)

THAI BEEF SALAD

(see page 81)

STEAMED RICE

(see page 30)

FRESH FRUIT

(see suggestions on page 180)

The day before, open the coconut, slice, and freeze any coconut slices not required. Keep the crisps for the lunchbox in a covered container in the refrigerator to cook the next day. Cook the steamed rice and let cool. Cook the beef to your taste, rare or medium, and let cool. Prepare all the ingredients for the beef salad and also the dressing. Place in separate covered containers and refrigerate overnight. Note that the recipes used serve four people, so you will need to adjust the quantities to serve just one.

7:20 AM — **HEAT** the oven and cook the coconut crisps.
7:25 — **MIX** all the salad ingredients and pour over the dressing.
7:40 — **WASH** the fresh fruit, if necessary. Remove the coconut crisps from the oven and let cool.
8:00 — **PACK** the beef salad, coconut crisps, rice, and fruit into suitable covered containers, and remember to pack a fork.

PREPARATION NOTES

SHAKE the coconut before you buy it to check that it is full of juice and not cracked. Use a food processor fitted with a sharp slicing blade to get really fine slices. **BUY** good quality filet mignon, organic if possible. This cut is known for its tenderness and leanness and is well suited to being pan-fried or broiled, as in this recipe. **BROIL** the beef to your taste. Leaving it to rest before slicing it helps the meat to stay juicy. **CUT** it as thinly as you can.

MIDWEEK LUNCH WITH FAMILY

THAI FRIED RICE

(see page 32)

BARBECUE SPARERIBS

(see page 166)

GREEN MANGO SALAD

(see page 97)

PINEAPPLE BUTTERFLIES

(see page 178)

TIME PLAN

Thai fried rice is a popular dish, with its many tastes and textures. It looks good served straight from the wok. Meaty spare ribs partner the rice perfectly, and the accompanying green mango salad has layers of delicious, spicy textures. Fresh pineapple butterflies round off a show-stopping meal.

The day before, make up the marinade for the spareribs. Cook the rice for the Thai fried rice, cool, and store in the refrigerator overnight in an airtight container.

AM
10:50 **PLACE** the spareribs in the marinade, making sure they are well coated, and refrigerate in a covered container.

11:00 **ASSEMBLE** and prepare all the ingredients for the fried rice. Cook the omelets, roll up, and set aside.

11:25 **ASSEMBLE** and prepare all the ingredients for the mango salad, including cutting the mango into shards.

11:45 **CUT** the pineapple into butterflies and cut suitably sized pieces of banana leaf to serve them on. Arrange on a serving dish.

PM
12:15 **PUT** the spareribs on a trivet in a pan, pour in water, and place in the oven. Make the mango salad, but toss it together only at the last minute.

12:55 **COOK** the Thai fried rice to the end of step 4.

1:15 **FINISH** the Thai rice and serve with the spareribs followed by salad.

1:45 **SERVE** the pineapple butterflies.

PREPARATION NOTES

COOK the rice for the Thai fried rice the day before the meal, so that you start with cold precooked rice, which gives the best result. **CHOOSE** the meatiest ribs you can find (some have scarcely any flesh on them). **BUY** the pineapple several days ahead to give it time to ripen and so develop its full flavor.

MIDWEEK LUNCH WITH FRIENDS

CHICKEN AND PORK SATAY

(see page 45)

KHUN NAN'S STEAMED FISH CURRY

(see page 113)

STEAMED RICE

(see page 30)

MIXED STIR-FRY VEGETABLES

(see page 89)

FRESH MANGO

(see page 178)

PREPARATION NOTES

CHECK whether you can buy a banana leaf. **CUT** out a couple of circles as described and blanch in boiling water. **PRACTICE** making the banana cups (see page 26), which are worth the effort.

TIME PLAN

Tender morsels of chicken and pork satay, served with a crunchy peanut sauce, make the perfect start to a meal that continues with a creamy steamed fish curry, fluffy fragrant rice, and crunchy stir-fried vegetables. Golden mango, presented Thai style, makes a refreshing desert.

The day before, cut the disks for the banana leaf cups, allowing two for each cup, and prepare the cups (see page 26). Slice the meats for the satay; cover and refrigerate.

10:40 AM
MAKE the peanut sauce and marinade for the satay. Pour the marinade over the meat slices. Soak some bamboo or wooden skewers.

11:20
PREPARE the fish and set in a covered container in the refrigerator. Make the curry mixture, cover, and keep cool. Prepare a garnish of shredded lime leaf and red chili. Set aside in a little coconut milk.

11:40
STEAM the rice. When cooked, leave it in the steamer or transfer to a bowl ready for reheating (see page 29), and set aside.

11:45
PREPARE the vegetables while the rice is steaming. Thread the chicken and pork pieces on to separate skewers.

12:05 PM
CUT the mangoes, cover, and chill.

12:25
FILL the banana cups at the last minute and secure in a steamer with crumpled foil to keep them steady (see recipe directions); alternatively use large ramekins. Start to cook as the guests arrive—the cups can be left in the steamer after cooking to keep warm.

1:00
COOK the stir-fry vegetables, reheat the rice, and serve. Serve the steamed curry garnished with coconut milk, lime leaf, and red chili.

1:15
COOK the satay and serve with the peanut sauce and cucumber salad.

1:45
SERVE the fresh mango.

WEEKEND LUNCH WITH FAMILY

SHRIMP TOASTS

(see page 38)

GREEN CHICKEN CURRY

(see page 105)

STEAMED RICE

(see page 30)

SPICY STRING BEANS

(see page 93)

GLUTINOUS RICE WITH MANGO SLICES

(see page 174)

TIME PLAN

Ever-popular shrimp toasts, crip and crunchy, are firm favorites. They look and taste fabulous. Classic green chicken curry, with its creamy coconut and green homemade curry paste, is memorable served with Thai fragrant rice and spicy crunchy beans.

The day before, soak the glutinous rice overnight or for 12 hours, then steam; prepare the coconut mixture, add the rice to absorb it, then cool and refrigerate in a covered container. Make the Thai relish.

AM 11:20 PREPARE the shrimp toasts and place on a tray lined with baking parchment paper. Cover loosely with plastic wrap and refrigerate.

11:50 SLICE the chicken and refrigerate in a container. Prepare all the green curry ingredients; keep the chicken refrigerated.

PM 12:15 ASSEMBLE the ingredients for the spicy beans.

12:25 STEAM the rice. When cooked, leave in the steamer or transfer to a bowl ready for reheating (see page 29), and set aside.

12:30 PEEL and slice the mango while the rice is cooking. Arrange the glutinous rice on plates with the mango and lime on top, cover lightly.

1:00 COOK the green chicken curry to the end of step 5.

1:15 COOK the shrimp toasts and serve with the Thai relish.

1:30 FINISH the chicken curry, reheat the rice, cook the beans, and serve.

2:00 SERVE the glutinous rice with mango slices.

PREPARATION NOTES

BUY the mangoes a few days before so they can ripen fully. LEAVE the cooked glutinous rice to stand in the coconut milk up to 2 hours so that it has time to absorb all the liquid. CUT the mango away from the pit very carefully, then PEEL and cut it lengthwise into attractive slices.

WEEKEND LUNCH WITH FRIENDS

MIXED SEAFOOD AND COCONUT SOUP
(see page 74)

RICE SALAD
(see page 31)

BARBECUE CHICKEN
(see page 169)

FRIED BANANAS
(see page 173)

PREPARATION NOTES

BUY the freshest fish you can find. **CHOOSE** chunky cod fillets, to produce satisfactory cubes. **SCORE** the squid flesh before cutting it into strips to help the flesh curl as it cooks. **CHOOSE** juicy, plump shrimp for the best flavor. **STORE** all the seafood in a covered container in the refrigerator.

TIME PLAN

Seafood in coconut soup zipped up with torn red chili puts the appetite on alert. The rice salad, a stunning display of separate ingredients on a large dish, is served with crisp barbecued chicken. Melt-in-the-mouth fried bananas, a Thai favorite, complete this lunch in style.

The day before, make the chili sauce to drizzle over the salad and store in a screwtop glass jar. Make the marinade for the chicken.

10:30 AM **PREPARE** the squid, assemble the fish, and refrigerate in a covered container. Prepare the coconut and turmeric for the soup.

11:15 **MARINADE** the chicken pieces in a glass or stainless steel container. Cover with plastic wrap, turning the pieces occasionally for an hour.

11:30 **ASSEMBLE** and prepare all the salad ingredients.

11:50 **ARRANGE** the salad ingredients around a mound of rice on a large serving dish with the dressing in a separate bowl or little pitcher.

12:00 PM **ASSEMBLE** the ingredients for the fried bananas.

12:15 **COOK** the chicken pieces.

12:30 **HEAT** the liquid ingredients for the soup with the spices and leaves. Add the coconut and turmeric mixture and the remaining ingredients. Set on one side.

1:20 **ADD** the fish to the soup once the guests are seated at the table.

1:35 **SERVE** the rice salad and sauce and the garnished barbecue chicken with the cucumber salad.

2:00 **COOK** and serve the fried bananas.

SIMPLE DINNER

TIME PLAN

Nibble on crunchy shrimp chips while waiting for steaming mussels cooked on a bed of fragrant herbs. The Thanying salad has crunchy vegetables and chicken, peanuts, and a sweet-sour-salty dressing, combining to make a memorable salad. Homemade coconut ice cream concludes this meal.

The day before, make the coconut milk ice cream. Cook the chicken for the salad, then cool and refrigerate it in a covered container. Halve all the recipe ingredients to prepare this meal for two.

PM 5:00   SCRUB the mussels, place in a large container, and cover with water until required. Make the chili sauce for the mussels.

5:30   ASSEMBLE all the ingredients for the salad, and blanch the beans. Dry-fry the sesame seeds. Pound the ingredients for the salad dressing.

6:15   STEAM the rice. When cooked, leave in the steamer or transfer to a bowl ready for reheating (see page 29), and set aside.

6:20   TOAST the dried coconut (unsweetened) to decorate the ice cream.

6:30   FRY the shrimp chips and drain well on paper towels. Make the sauce or relish.

7:00   TOSS the cucumber, dressing ingredients, and peanuts together, then fold in the remaining ingredients and cover with plastic wrap. Put the coconut ice cream in the refrigerator to soften.

7:15   SERVE the shrimp chips.

7:25   COOK the mussels. Lift on to serving plates, discard the herbs, and add the sauce to the juices in the wok. Heat and pour over the mussels. Garnish with basil leaves. Place a separate bowl in the center of the table for the mussel shells.

7:40   SERVE the salad garnished with cilantro and sesame seeds, with lettuce and rice.

8:00   SERVE the coconut milk ice cream.

ROMANTIC DINNER

The prettiest do-it-yourself appetizer, full of color and texture, is followed by indulgent scallops with a kick of chili, fluffy steamed rice, crunchy baby corn, and sugar snap peas. A golden, cooling sherbet ends the meal.

LETTUCE PACKAGES

(see page 58)

STIR-FRY SCALLOPS WITH CHILI AND BASIL LEAVES

(see page 134)

STEAMED RICE

(see page 30)

BABY CORN AND SUGAR SNAPS WITH GINGER AND GARLIC

(see page 86)

MANGO SHERBET

(see page 185)

The day before, make the mango sherbet. Put the scallops in a container in the refrigerator to thaw, if frozen. Halve all the recipe ingredients to prepare this meal for two.

PM
6:00 ASSEMBLE and prepare the ingredients for the stir-fry scallops. Prepare the ingredients for the lettuce packages.
6:30 STEAM the rice. When cooked, leave in the steamer or transfer to a bowl ready for reheating (see page 29), and set aside.
6:35 ASSEMBLE and prepare the ingredients for the baby corn stir-fry while the rice is cooking.
7:00 TAKE the sherbet out of the freezer. Place in the refrigerator to soften.
7:45 SERVE the lettuce package ingredients, for each person to assemble.
8:00 REHEAT the rice while stir-frying the vegetables. Put in warm dishes, then stir-fry the scallops, and serve.
8:30 SERVE the mango sherbet decorated with lime shreds.

PREPARATION NOTES

CHOOSE fresh scallops that are pale beige to creamy pink. (You may need to order them in advance, or at least check when they will be in stock.) Frozen scallops tend to be whiter in colour. THAW frozen ones overnight in a covered container in the refrigerator. COOK the scallops only until they turn opaque, which means they are done. Longer cooking will only toughen them, spoiling their delicate taste and texture.

MIDWEEK DINNER WITH FAMILY

SHRIMP IN BLANKETS

(see page 49)

NORTHERN THAI CURRY WITH PORK AND GINGER

(see page 102)

STEAMED RICE

(see page 30)

STIR-FRY BROCCOLI AND CARROTS WITH BEAN CURD AND PEANUTS

(see page 90)

PUMPKIN FILLED WITH COCONUT CUSTARD

(see page 182)

TIME PLAN

Delicious, crispy-wrapped shrimp with a chili sauce are followed by a slow-cooked flavorsome pork curry, crunchy stir-fried vegetables, and steamed fragrant rice. The stunning dessert, with its creamy coconut custard in a pumpkin, adds a triumphant note.

The day before, prepare the stuffing for the shrimp in blankets and thaw the wrappers. Make the curry, so that the flavors develop. Prepare and steam the coconut custard in pumpkin. Cool and place in a deep dish or bowl using foil straps. Cover and refrigerate.

PM

5:50 MAKE the shrimp in blankets.

6:00 STEAM the rice. When cooked, leave in the steamer or transfer to a bowl ready for reheating (see page 29), and set aside.

6:05 PREPARE the broccoli for the stir-fry and cut the carrot as directed while the rice is cooking. Blanch the broccoli; when cold, refrigerate in a covered container.

6:15 ASSEMBLE and prepare the sauce ingredients for the vegetables. Chop the pork crackling and ginger into matchstick pieces for the curry garnish.

6:30 MAKE the sauce for the shrimp in blankets. Turn the curry into a saucepan or casserole to reheat slowly on top of the stove.

6:45 TAKE the pumpkin out of the container. Cut into wedges and arrange on a serving dish with some fresh fruit, if liked. Cover with plastic wrap.

7:15 COOK and serve the shrimp with the dipping sauce. Reheat the rice.

7:30 STIR-FRY the vegetables, add the sauce and bean curd. Serve the curry garnished with pork crackling and ginger, the rice, and the stir-fry vegetables topped with peanuts.

8:00 SERVE the sliced pumpkin with coconut custard.

MIDWEEK DINNER WITH FRIENDS

TIME PLAN

The subtle flavors of the soup are complemented by the colorful and delicious shrimp and pineapple curry and stir-fry beef with broccoli and oyster sauce. Finish with oranges, lychees, and mango in a flower-perfumed syrup.

The day before, make up the syrup for the dessert and chill. Make the chicken stock for the soup or thaw. Thaw frozen shrimp in a covered container in the refrigerator. Make the stuffing for the mushrooms.

PM
5:00 SOAK the mushrooms, if using Chinese, and remove the stems. Stuff the mushrooms of choice and leave in the refrigerator.

5:15 ASSEMBLE and prepare the fruits for the dessert. Chill, covered, in the refrigerator. Crush the partly thawed ice in a food processor and place in a wide box in one layer in the freezer until just before the meal.

5:45 ASSEMBLE the ingredients for the curry. Make the soup to the end of step 3. Prepare all the ingredients for the beef with broccoli. Blanch the broccoli.

6:15 ASSEMBLE and prepare the green vegetables for the stir-fry and make the yellow bean sauce. Place the mushrooms in a steamer.

6:30 STEAM the rice. When cooked, leave in the steamer or transfer to a bowl ready for reheating (see page 29), and set aside.

6:35 POUR the chilled syrup over the fruits in a bowl for dessert while the rice is cooking and move the crushed ice to the refrigerator ready to spoon on top at the last minute with some orchid flowers.

6.45 COOK the curry to step 3. Steam the mushrooms and simmer the soup. Add the remaining soup ingredients, then serve the soup.

7:30 STIR-FRY the beef with broccoli. Finish the curry, reheat the rice, cook the egg noodles (to accompany the beef dish), and stir-fry the green leaves and yellow bean sauce. Serve these dishes.

8:00 SERVE the exotic fruits with syrup and crushed ice.

DINNER PARTY

TIME PLAN

Spicy fish cakes, delicate wonton soup, creamy mixed vegetable curry, fluffy fragrant rice, and a deep-flavored Mussaman curry are complemented by the sweet-sour-salty salad. Beautiful Thai rubies add the finishing touch.

The day before, make up the chicken stock for the soup or thaw if frozen. Make the filling for the wontons, cover, and refrigerate. Make up the Mussaman curry to the end of step 5, cool, cover, and refrigerate. Make the Thai fish cakes (three per person) and dipping sauce and refrigerate. If you are serving eight, double all the quantities.

PM

4:15 **THAW** the wrappers and make up the wontons (three per person).
4:40 **TAKE** the Mussaman curry out of the refrigerator. Make the red rubies and put in ice water. Make the sweetened coconut milk, pour into a pitcher, cover, and chill.
5:25 **STEAM** the rice. When cooked, leave in the steamer or transfer to a bowl ready for reheating (see page 29), and set aside.
5:30 **ASSEMBLE** and prepare all the ingredients for the vegetable curry while the rice is cooking. Cook to the end of step 2.
6:00 **ASSEMBLE** and prepare all the ingredients for the salad. Make up the salad to the end of step 2. Have the tomatoes, papaya, or cabbage ready to complete the salad. Soak the tamarind pulp, then strain.
6:30 **REHEAT** the Mussaman curry gently in a flameproof casserole on top of the stove. Add the final seasonings when hot.
6:40 **FINISH** the vegetable curry.
7:15 **COOK** the fish cakes and serve with the crunchy dipping sauce.
7:30 **COOK** the wontons, heat the stock, serve the soup, and reheat the rice.
7:45 **GARNISH** the Mussaman curry, then serve with the vegetable curry and rice. Toss the final salad ingredients together, garnish, and serve.
8:15 **SERVE** the Thai rubies.

COCKTAIL PARTY

TIME PLAN

This varied selection of Thai delights comprises soft dumplings and money bags, crisp egg rolls, crunchy coconut crisps and shrimp chips, spicy nam prik sauce with crudités, and satay prawns with peanut sauce.

The day before, open the coconut and make the coconut slices, put in a plastic container in the refrigerator. Make the nam prik sauce and money bag filling and refrigerate. This menu will feed eight to ten guests.

PM
3:00 MAKE the filling for the Thai egg rolls and thaw the wrappers.
3:30 MAKE the filling for the dumplings and thaw the wrappers, including those for the money bags.
4:00 MAKE the marinade for the shrimp, and marinate. Soak the skewers.
4:30 DEEP-FRY the shrimp chips, drain well on paper towels. Put in a bowl and pour the dipping sauces into small dishes. Have deep oil in a pan or wok on one side to be ready for deep-frying later.
5:00 PREPARE the Thai egg rolls and money bags and place on a floured plate. Make the dumplings and place on nonstick baking parchment paper in steamer baskets ready for cooking.
5:45 CUT the vegetables into finger-like pieces to serve with the nam prik sauce. Arrange on plates with the nam prik sauce in a bowl and garnish with cilantro. Cover with plastic wrap and keep in a cool place.
6:00 HEAT the oven, spread the coconut slices on a baking sheet, and cook in the oven until golden. Transfer to bowls. Thread the shrimp on the skewers. Set on a piece of foil ready to put in a broiler pan to cook. Put the peanut sauce into a pan to reheat later. Make the cucumber salad unless serving with triangles of toast and chunks of cucumber.
6:50 PLACE the wok or deep pan of oil next to the stove. Set the dumplings in a steamer. Have the kettle ready to boil.
7:30 COOK the snacks and serve with the sauces and relishes.

INDEX